ETHICS WITHOUT GOD

To Kurt Neureither

Ethics Without God

KAI NIELSEN

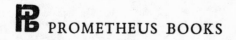
PROMETHEUS BOOKS

First published 1973 by Pemberton Books
(Pemberton Publishing Co Ltd), 88 Islington
High Street, London N1 8EN
and Prometheus Books
1203 Kensington Avenue
Buffalo, New York 14215

SBN (UK and World)
    301 73021 2 *boards*
    301 73022 0 *paper*

SBN (US and Canada)
    0 87975 014 6 *cloth*
    0 87975 019 7 *paper*

Printed in Great Britain by
Richard Clay (The Chaucer Press) Ltd,
Bungay, Suffolk

PREFACE

Many people have helped me in various ways in the writing of this book. Foremost is the help that I have received from several generations of students in discussing these issues at Amherst College, Harpur College, New York University and the University of Calgary. They have taught me much more than they may have realized. Professor Patterson Brown, who initially was one of those students, by forcefully and perceptively opposing the view I have articulated in Chapters One and Two, forced on me refinements for which I would not otherwise have seen the need; I am deeply indebted to him. I also owe a debt of gratitude to my wife, Elisabeth Nielsen, for helping me in many ways, great and small, and particularly for her persistent criticism of what she took to be (and indeed still takes to be) the wrongheaded direction of the last chapter. Finally, I should like to thank Kurt Neureither, Pamela Long, Beverly Forbes and Eileen Markson for their considerable help in preparing and delivering the manuscript.

Kai Nielsen,
Calgary, Alberta,
Canada
November 1972

CONTENTS

ONE

MORALITY AND THE WILL OF GOD

I

IT IS THE CLAIM of many influential Jewish and Christian theologians (Brunner, Buber, Barth, Niebuhr and Bultmann —to take outstanding examples) that the only genuine basis for morality is in religion. And any old religion is not good enough. The only truly adequate foundation for moral belief is a religion that acknowledges the absolute sovereignty of the Lord found in the prophetic religions.

These theologians will readily grant what is plainly true, namely, that as a matter of fact many non-religious people behave morally, but they contend that without a belief in God and his law there is no ground or reason for being moral. The sense of moral relativism, scepticism and nihilism rampant in our age is due in large measure to the general weakening of religious belief in an age of science. Without God there can be no objective foundation for our moral beliefs. As Brunner puts it,[1] 'The believer alone clearly perceives that the Good, as it is recognized in faith, is the sole Good, and all that is otherwise called good cannot lay claim to this title, at least in the ultimate sense of the word ... The Good consists in always doing what God wills at any particular moment.' Moreover, this moral Good can only be attained by our 'unconditional obedience' to God, the ground of our being. Without God life would have no point and morality would have no basis. Without religious belief, without the Living God, there could be no adequate answer to the persistently gnawing questions: What ought we to do? How ought I to live?

Is this frequently repeated claim justified? Are our moral

beliefs and conceptions based on or grounded in a belief in the God of Judaism, Christianity and Islam? In trying to come to grips with this question, we need to ask ourselves three fundamental questions.

(1) Is being willed by God the, or even a, *fundamental* criterion for that which is so willed being morally good or for its being something that ought to be done?

(2) Is being willed by God the *only* criterion for that which is so willed being morally good or for its being something that ought to be done?

(3) Is being willed by God the only *adequate* criterion for that which is so willed being morally good or being something that ought to be done?

I shall argue that the fact that God wills something—if indeed that is a fact—cannot be a fundamental criterion for its being morally good or obligatory and thus it cannot be the only criterion or the only adequate criterion for moral goodness or obligation.

By way of preliminaries we should first get clear what is meant by a fundamental criterion. When we speak of the criterion for the goodness of an action or attitude we speak of some measure or test by virtue of which we may decide which actions or attitudes are good or desirable, or, at least, are the least undesirable of the alternate actions or attitudes open to us. A moral criterion is the measure we use for determining the value or worth of an action, principle, rule or attitude. We have such a measure or test when we have some generally relevant considerations by which we may decide whether something is whatever it is said to be. A fundamental moral criterion is (*a*) a test or measure used to judge the legitimacy of moral rules and/or acts or attitudes, and (*b*) a measure that one would give up last if one were reasoning morally. (In reality, there probably is no single fundamental criterion, although there are fundamental criteria.)

There is a further preliminary matter we need to consider.

In asking about the basis or authority for our moral beliefs we are not asking about how we came to have them. If you ask someone where he got his moral beliefs, he, to be realistic, should answer that he got them from his parents, parent surrogates, teachers.[2] They are beliefs which he has been conditioned to accept. But the validity or soundness of a belief is independent of its origin. When one person naïvely asks another where he got his moral beliefs, most likely he is not asking how he came by them, but rather, (a) on what authority he holds these beliefs, or (b) what good reasons or justification he has for these moral beliefs. He should answer that he does not and cannot hold these beliefs on any authority. It is indeed true that many of us turn to people for moral advice and guidance in moral matters, but if we do what we do simply because it has been authorized, we cannot be reasoning and acting as moral agents; for to respond as a moral agent, one's moral principle must be something which is subscribed to by one's own deliberate commitment, and it must be something for which one is prepared to give reasons.

Keeping these preliminary clarifications in mind, we can return to my claim that the fact (if indeed it is a fact) that God has commanded, willed or ordained something cannot, in the very nature of the case, be a fundamental criterion for claiming that whatever is commanded, willed or ordained *ought* to be done.

II

Some perceptive remarks made by A. C. Ewing will carry us part of the way.[3] Theologians like Barth and Brunner claim that ethical principles gain their justification because they are God's decrees. But as Ewing points out, if 'being obligatory' means just 'willed by God', it becomes unintelligible to ask why God wills one thing rather than another. In fact, there can be no reason for his willing one thing rather than another, for his willing it *eo ipso* makes whatever it is he wills good, right or obligatory. 'God wills it because it ought to be done' becomes 'God wills it because God wills it'; but the first sentence, even as used by the most ardent believer, is not a tautology. 'If it were said in reply that God's commands determine what we ought to do but that these commands were only issued because it was good that they should be or because obedience to them did good, this would still make judgments about the good, at least, independent of the will of God, and we should not have given a definition of all fundamental ethical concepts in terms of God or made ethics dependent on God.'[4] Furthermore, it becomes senseless to say what the believer very much wants to say, namely, 'I ought always to do what God wills' if 'what I ought to do' and 'what God wills' have the same meaning. And to say I ought to do what God wills because I love God makes the independent assumption that I ought to love God and that I ought to do what God wills if I love him.

Suppose we say instead that we ought to do what God wills because God will punish us if we do not obey him. This may indeed be a cogent self-interested or prudential reason for doing what God commands, but it is hardly a morally good reason for doing what he commands since such considerations of self-interest cannot be an adequate basis for morality. A powerful being—an omnipotent and omniscient being—speaking out of the whirlwind cannot by his mere commands create an obligation. Ewing goes on to assert: 'Without a prior conception of God as good or his commands as right, God would have no more claim on our obedience than Hitler or Stalin except that he would have more power than even they had to make things uncomfortable for those who disobey him.'[5] Unless we assume that God is morally perfect, unless we assume the perfect goodness of God, there can be no necessary 'relation between being commanded or willed by God and being obligatory or good'.[6]

To this it is perfectly correct to reply that as believers we must believe that God is wholly and completely good, the most perfect of all conceivable beings.[7] It is not open for a Jew or a Christian to question the goodness of God. He must start with that assumption. Any man who seriously questions God's goodness or asks why he should obey God's commands shows by this very response that he is not a Jew or a Christian. Believers must claim that God is wholly and utterly good and that what he wills or commands is of necessity good, though this does not entail that the believer is claiming that the necessity here is a logical necessity. For a believer, God is all good; he is the perfect good. This being so, it would seem that the believer is justified in saying that he and we—if his claim concerning God is correct—ought to do what God wills and that our morality is after all grounded in a belief in God. But this claim of his is clearly dependent on his assumption that God is good. Yet I shall argue that even if God is good, indeed, even if God is the perfect good, it does not follow that morality can be based on religion and that we can know what we ought to do simply by knowing what God wishes us to do.

III

To come to understand the grounds for this last rather elliptical claim, we must consider the logical status of 'God is good.' Is it a non-analytic and in some way substantive claim, or is it analytic? (Can we say that it is neither?) No matter what we say, we get into difficulties.

Let us first try to claim that it is non-analytic, that it is in some way a substantive statement. So understood, God cannot then be by definition good. If the statement is synthetic and substantive, its denial cannot be self-contradictory; that is, it cannot be self-contradictory to assert that X is God but X is not good. It would always in fact be wrong to assert this, for God is the perfect good, but the denial of this claim is not self-contradictory, it is just false or in some way mistaken. The 'is' in 'God is the perfect good' is not the 'is' of identity, perfect goodness is being predicated of God in some logically contingent way. It is the religious experience of the believer and the events recorded in the Bible that lead the believer to the steadfast conviction that God has a purpose or vocation for him which he can fulfil only by completely submitting to God's will. God shall lead him and guide him in every thought, word and deed. Otherwise he will be like a man shipwrecked, lost in a vast and indifferent universe. Through careful attention to the Bible, he comes to understand that God is a wholly good being who has dealt faithfully with his chosen people. God is not by definition perfectly good or even good, but in reality, though not of logical necessity, he never falls short of perfection.

Assuming that 'God is good' is not a truth of language, how, then, do we know that God is good? Do we know or have good grounds for believing that the remarks made at the end of the above paragraph are so? The believer can indeed make such a claim, but how do we or how does he know that this is so? What grounds have we for believing that God is good? Naïve people, recalling how God spoke to Job out of the whirlwind may say that God is good because he is omnipotent and omniscient. But this clearly will not do, for, as Hepburn points out, there is nothing logically improper about saying 'X is omnipotent and omniscient and morally wicked.'[8] Surely in the world as we know it there is no logical connection between being powerful and knowledgeable and being good. As far as I can see, all that God proved to Job when he spoke to him out of the whirlwind was that God was an immeasurably powerful being; but he did not prove his moral superiority to Job and he did nothing at all even to exhibit his moral goodness. (One might even argue that he exhibited moral wickedness.) We need not assume that omnipotence and omniscience bring with them goodness or even wisdom.

What other reason could we have for claiming that God is

good? We might say that he is good because he tells us to do good in thought, word and deed and to love one another. In short, in his life and in his precepts God exhibits for us his goodness and love. Now one might argue that children's hospitals and concentration camps clearly show that such a claim is false. But let us assume that in some way God does exhibit his goodness to man. Let us assume that if we examine God's works we cannot but affirm that God is good.[9] We come to understand that he is not cruel, callous or indifferent. But in order to make such judgments or to gain such an understanding, we must use our own logically independent moral criteria. In taking God's goodness as not being true by definition or as being some kind of conceptual truth, we have, in asserting 'God is good', of necessity made a moral judgment, a moral appraisal, using a criterion that cannot be based on a knowledge that God exists or that he issues commands. We call God good because we have experienced the goodness of his acts, but in order to do this, in order to know that he is good or to have any grounds for believing that he is good, we must have an independent moral criterion which we use in making this predication of God. So if 'God is good' is taken to be synthetic and substantive, then morality cannot simply be based on a belief in God. We must of logical necessity have some criterion of goodness that is not derived from any statement asserting that there is a deity.

IV

Let us alternatively, and more plausibly, take 'God is good' to be a truth of language. Now some truths of language (some analytic statements) are statements of identity, such as 'puppies are young dogs' or 'a father is a male parent.' Such statements are definitions and the 'is' indicates identity. But 'God is good' is clearly not such a statement of identity, for that 'God' does not have the same meaning as 'good' can easily be seen from the following case: Jane says to Betsy, after

Betsy helps an old lady across the street, 'That was good of you.' 'That was good of you' most certainly does not mean 'that was God of you.' And when we say 'conscientiousness is good' we do not mean to say 'conscientiousness is God.' To say, as a believer does, that God is good is not to say that God is God. This clearly indicates that the word God does not have the same meaning as the word good. When we are talking about God we are not talking simply about morality.

'God is the perfect good' is somewhat closer to 'a father is a male parent', but even here 'God' and 'the perfect good' are not identical in meaning. 'God is the perfect good' in some important respects is like 'a triangle is a trilateral.' Though something is a triangle if and only if it is a trilateral, it does not follow that 'triangle' and 'trilateral' have the same meaning. Similarly, something is God if and only if that something is the perfect good, but it does not follow that 'God' and 'the perfect good' have the same meaning. When we speak of God we wish to say other things about him as well, though indeed what is true of God will also be true of the perfect good. Yet what is true of the evening star will also be true of the morning star since they both refer to the same object, namely Venus, but, as Frege has shown, it does not follow that the two terms have the same meaning if they have the same referent

Even if it could be made out that 'God is the perfect good' is in some way a statement of identity, (*a*) it would not make 'God is good' a statement of identity, and (*b*) we could know that X is the perfect good only if we already knew how to decide that X is good.[10] So even on the assumption that 'God is the perfect good' is a statement of identity, we need an independent way of deciding whether something is good; we must have an independent criterion for goodness.

Surely the alternative presently under consideration is more plausible than the alternative considered in section III. 'God is good' most certainly appears to be analytic in the way 'puppies are young', 'a bachelor is unmarried' or 'unjustified killing is wrong' are analytic. These statements are not statements of identity; they are not definitions, though they all follow from definitions and to deny any of them is self-contradictory.

In short, it seems to me correct to maintain that 'God is good', 'puppies are young' and 'triangles are three-sided' are all truths of language; the predicates partially define their subjects. That is to say—to adopt for a moment a Platonic sounding idiom—goodness is partially definitive of Godhood, as youngness is partially definitive of puppyhood and as three-sidedness is partially definitive of triangularity.

To accept this is not at all to claim that we can have no understanding of good without an understanding of God; and the truth of the above claim that God is good will not show that God is the, or even a, fundamental criterion for goodness. Let us establish first that and then how the fact of such truths of language does not show that we could have no understanding of good without having an understanding of God. We could not understand the full religious sense of what is meant by God without knowing that whatever is denoted by this term is said to be good; but, as 'young' or 'three-sided' are understood without reference to puppies or triangles though the converse cannot be the case, so 'good' is also understood quite independently of any reference to God. We can intelligibly say, 'I have a three-sided figure here that is most certainly not a triangle' and 'colts are young but they are not puppies.' Similarly, we can well say 'conscientiousness, under most circumstances at least, is good even in a world without God.' Such an utterance is clearly intelligible, to believer and non-believer alike. It is a well-formed English sentence with a use in the language. Here we can use the word good without either asserting or assuming the reality of God. Such linguistic evidence clearly shows that good is a concept which can be understood quite independently of any reference to the deity, that morality without religion, without theism, is quite possible. In fact, just the reverse is the case. Christianity, Judaism and theistic religions of that sort could not exist if people did not have a moral understanding that was, logically speaking, quite independent of such religions. We could have no understanding of the truth of 'God is good' or of the concept God unless we had an independent understanding of goodness.

That this is so can be seen from the following considerations. If we had no understanding of the word young, and if we did not know the criteria for deciding whether a dog was young, we could not know how correctly to apply the word puppy. Without such a prior understanding of what it is to be young, we could not understand the sentence 'puppies are young.' Similarly, if we had no understanding of the use of the word good, and if we did not know the criteria for deciding whether a being (or if you will, a power or a force) was good, we could not know how correctly to apply the word God. Without such a prior understanding of goodness, we could not understand the sentence 'God is good.' This clearly shows that our understanding of morality and knowledge of goodness are independent of any knowledge that we may or may not have of the divine. Indeed, without a prior and logically independent understanding of good and without some non-religious criterion for judging something to be good, the religious person could have no knowledge of God, for he could not know whether that powerful being who spoke out of the whirlwind and laid the foundations of the earth was in fact worthy of worship and perfectly good.

From my argument we should conclude that we cannot decide whether something is good or whether it ought to be done simply from finding out (assuming that we can find out) that God commanded it, willed it, enjoined it. Furthermore, whether 'God is good' is synthetic (substantive) or analytic (a truth of language), the concept of good must be understood as something distinct from the concept of God; that is to say, a man could know how to use 'good' properly and still not know how to use 'God'. Conversely, a man could not know how to use 'God' correctly unless he already understood how to use 'good'. An understanding of goodness is logically prior to, and is independent of, any understanding or acknowledgment of God.

V

In attempting to counter my argument for the necessary independence of morality—including a central facet of religious morality—from any beliefs about the existence or powers of the deity, the religious moralist might begin by conceding that (*a*) there are secular moralities that are logically independent of religion, and (*b*) that we must understand the meanings of moral terms independently of understanding what it means to speak of God. He might even go so far as to grant that only a man who understood what good and bad were could come to believe in God. 'Good', he might grant, does not mean 'willed by God' or anything like that; and 'there is no God, but human happiness is nonetheless good' is indeed perfectly intelligible as a moral utterance. But granting that, it is still the case that Jew and Christian do and must—on pain of ceasing to be Jew or Christian—take God's will as their final court of appeal in the making of moral appraisals or judgments. Any rule, act or attitude that conflicts with what the believer sincerely believes to be the will of God must be rejected by him. It is indeed true that in making moral judgments the Jew or Christian does not always use God's will as a criterion for what is good or what ought to be done. When he says 'fluoridation is a good thing' or 'the resumption of nuclear testing is a crime', he need not be using God's will as a criterion for his moral judgment. But where any moral judgment or any other moral criterion conflicts with God's ordinances, or with what the person making the judgment honestly takes to be God's ordinances, he must accept those ordinances, or he is no longer a Jew or a Christian. This acceptance is a crucial test of his faith. In this way, God's will is his fundamental moral criterion.

That the orthodox Jew or Christian would reason in this way is perfectly true, but though he says that God's will is his fundamental criterion, it is still plain that he has a yet more fundamental criterion which he must use in order to employ God's will as a moral criterion. Such a religious moralist must believe and thus be prepared to make the moral claim that there exists a being whom he deems to be perfectly good or worthy of worship and whose will should always be obeyed. But to do this he must have a moral criterion (a standard for what is morally good) that is independent of God's will or what people believe to be God's will. In fact, the believer's moral criterion—'because it is willed by God'— is in logical dependence on some distinct criterion in virtue of which the believer judges that something is perfectly good, is worthy of worship. And in making this very crucial judgment he cannot appeal to God's will as a criterion, for, that there is a being worthy of the appellation 'God', depends in. part on the above prior moral claim. Only if it is correct, can we justifiably say that there is a God.

It is crucial to keep in mind that 'a wholly good being exists who is worthy of worship' is not analytic is not a truth of language, though 'God is wholly good' is. The former is rather a substantive moral statement (expressing a moral judgment) and a very fundamental one indeed, for the believer's whole faith rests on it. Drop this and everything goes.

It is tempting to reply to my above argument in this vein: 'but it is blasphemy to judge God; no account of the logical structure of the believer's argument can be correct if it says that the believer must judge that God is good.' Here we must beware of verbal magic and attend very carefully to precisely what it is we are saying. I did not—and could not on pain of contradiction—say that God must be judged worthy of worship, perfectly good; for God by definition is worthy of worship, perfectly good. I said something quite different, namely that the believer and non-believer alike must decide whether there exists or could conceivably exist a force, a being ('ground of being') that is worthy of worship or perfectly good; and I further said that in deciding this, one makes a moral judgment that can in no way be logically dependent on God's will. Rather, the moral standard, 'because it is willed by God', is dependent for its validity on the acceptance of the claim that there is a being worthy of worship. And as our little word 'worthy' indicates, this is unequivocally a moral judgment for believer and non-believer alike.

There is a rather more baroque objection[11] to my argument that (a) nothing could count as the Judaeo-Christian God unless that reality is worthy of worship and (b) it is our own moral insight that must tell us if anything at all is or ever possibly could be worthy of worship or whether there is a being who possesses perfect goodness. My conclusion from (a) and (b) was that rather than morality being based on religion, it can be seen that religion in a very fundamental sense must be based on morality. The counter-argument claims that such a conclusion is premature because the judgment that something is worthy of worship is not a moral judgment; it is an evaluative judgment, a religious evaluation, but not a moral judgment. The grounds for this counter-claim are that if the judgment is a moral judgment, as I assumed, then demono-latry—the worship of evil spirits—would be self-contra-dictory. But although demonolatry is morally and religiously perverse, it is not self-contradictory. Hence my argument must be mistaken.

However, if we say 'Z is worthy of worship' or that, given Judaeo-Christian attitudes, 'if Z is what ought to be wor-shipped then Z must be good', it does not follow that

demonolatry is self-contradictory or incoherent. Not everyone uses language as Jews and Christians do and not everyone
shares the conventions of those religious groups. To say that
nothing can be God, the Judaeo-Christian God, unless it is
worthy of worship, and to affirm that the judgment of something as worthy of worship is a moral judgment, is not to
deny that some people on some grounds could judge that
what they believe to be evil spirits are worthy of worship. By
definition, they could not be Jews or Christians—they show
by their linguistic behaviour that they do not believe in the
Judaeo-Christian God who, by definition, is perfectly good.
Jews and Christians recognize that believers in demonolatry
do not believe in God but in evil spirits whom such Joycean
characters judge to be worthy of worship. The Christian and
the demonolater make different moral judgments of a very
fundamental sort reflecting different views of the world.

VI

The dialectic of our general argument about morality and
divine commands should not end here. There are some further
considerations which need to be brought to the forefront.
Consider the theological claim that there is an infinite self-
existent being, upon whom all finite realities depend for their
existence, but who in turn depends on nothing. Assuming the
intelligibility of the key concepts in this claim and assuming
also that we know this claim to be true, it still needs to be
asked how we can know, except by the use of our own moral
understanding, that this infinite, self-existent being is good
or is a being whose commands we ought to obey. Since he—
to talk about this being anthropomorphically by the use of
personal pronouns—is powerful enough, we might decide
that it would be 'the better part of valour' to obey him, but
this decision would not at all entail that we ought to obey him.
How do we know that this being is good, except by our own
moral discernment? We could not discover that this being is

good or just by discovering that he 'laid the foundation of the world' or 'created man in his image and likeness'. No information about the behaviour patterns of this being would of itself tell us that he was good, righteous or just. We ourselves would have to decide that, or, to use the misleading idiom of the ethical intuitionist, we would have to intuit or somehow come to perceive or understand that the unique ethical properties of goodness, righteousness and justness apply to this strange being or 'ground of all being' that we somehow discover to exist. Only if we independently knew what we would count as good, righteous, just, would we be in a position to know whether this being is good or whether his commands ought to be obeyed. That most Christians most of the time unquestionably assume that he is good only proves that this judgment is for them a fundamental moral judgment. But this should hardly be news.

At this point it is natural to reply: 'Still, we would not even call this being God unless he was thought to be good. God, whatever else he may or may not be, is a fitting or proper object of worship.' A person arguing thus might continue: 'This is really a material mode statement about the use of the word God; that is to say, we would not call Z God unless that Z were a fitting or proper object of worship or a being that ought to be worshipped. And if we say "Z is a fitting object of worship" or "Z ought to be worshipped" we must also be prepared to say "Z is good". Z could not be one without being the other; and if Z is a fitting object of worship, Z necessarily is a being we would call God. Thus, if Z is called God, then Z must also of necessity be called good since in Judaeo-Christian contexts what ought to be worshipped must also be good. [This is a logical remark about the use of the phrase "ought to be worshipped" in Judaeo-Christian contexts.] God, by definition, is good. Though the word God is not equivalent to the word good, we would not call a being or power "God" unless that being was thought to be good.'

The above point is well taken, but it still remains the case that the believer has not derived a moral claim from a non-moral religious one. Rather, he has only indicated that the word God, like the words Saint, Santa Claus, Hunky, Nigger, Mick or Kike, is not a purely descriptive term. 'God', like 'Saint', etc, has an evaluative force; it expresses a pro-attitude on the part of the believer and does not just designate or even describe a necessary being or transcendent power or immanent force. Such a believer—unlike Schopenhauer—means by 'God' something toward which he has an appropriate pro-attitude; employing this word with its usual evaluative force, he could not say, 'God commands it but it is really evil to do it.' If, on the other hand, we simply think of what is purportedly designated or described by the word God—the descriptive force of the word—we can say, for example, without paradox, 'an objective power commands it but it is evil to do it.' By simply considering the reality allegedly denoted by the word 'God', we cannot discover whether this 'reality' is good. If we simply let Z stand for this reality, we can always ask, 'Is it good?' This is never a self-answering question in the way it is if we ask, 'Is murder evil?' Take away the evaluative force of the word God and you have no ground for claiming that it must be the case that God is good; to make this claim, with our admittedly fallible moral understanding, we must decide if this Z is good.

'But'—it will be countered—'you have missed the significance of the very point you have just made. As you say yourself, "God" is not just a descriptive word and God-sentences are not by any means used with a purely descriptive aim. "God" normally has an evaluative use and God-sentences have a directive force. You cannot begin to understand them if you do not take this into consideration. You cannot just consider what Z designates or purports to designate.'

My reply to this is that we can and must if we are going to attain clarity in these matters. Certain crucial and basic sentences like 'God created the Heavens and the earth' and 'God is in Christ', are by no means just moral or practical utterances and they would not have the evaluative force they do if it were not thought that in some strange way they described a mysterious objective power. The religious quest is a quest to find a Z such that Z is worthy of worship. This being the case, the evaluative force of the words and of the utterance is dependent on the descriptive force. How else but by our own moral judgment that Z is a being worthy to be worshipped are we enabled to call this Z 'my Lord and my God'? Christians say there is a Z such that Z should be worshipped. Non-believers deny this or remain sceptical. Findlay,[12] for example, points out that his atheism is in part moral because he does not believe that there can possibly be a Z such that Z is a worthy object of worship. Father Copleston,[13] on the other hand, says there is a Z such that Z ought to be worshipped. This Z, Father Copleston claims, is a 'necessary being' whose non-existence is in some important sense inconceivable. But both Findlay and Copleston are using their own moral understanding in making their respective moral judgments. Neither is deriving or deducing his moral judgment from the statement 'there is a Z' or from noticing or adverting to the fact—if it is a fact—that Z is 'being-itself', 'a reality whose non-existence is unthinkable', 'the ground of being' or the like.

Morality cannot be based on religion. If anything, the opposite is partly true, for nothing can be God unless he or it is an object worthy of worship and it is our own moral insight that must tell us if anything at all could possibly be worthy of worship.

It is true that if some Z is God, then, by definition, Z is an object worthy of worship. But this does not entail there is such a Z; that there is such a Z would depend both on what is the case and on what we, as individuals, judge to be worthy of worship. 'God is worthy of worship' is—for most uses of

'God'—analytic. To understand this sentence requires no insight at all but only a knowledge of English; but that there is or can be a Z such that Z is worthy of worship depends, in part at least, on the moral insight—or lack thereof—of that fallible creature that begins and ends in dust.

In her puzzling article, 'Modern Moral Philosophy',[14] Miss Anscombe has made a different sort of objection to the type of approach taken here. Moral uses of obligation statements, she argues, have no reasonable sense outside a divine-law conception of ethics. Without God, such conceptions are without sense. There was once a context, a religious way of life, in which these conceptions had a genuine application. 'Ought' was once equated, in the relevant context, with 'being obliged', 'bound' or 'required'. This came about because of the influence of the Torah. Because of the 'dominance of Christianity for many centuries the concepts of being bound, permitted or excused became deeply embedded in our language and thought.'[15] But since this is no longer so unequivocally the case these conceptions have become rootless. Shorn of this theistic Divine Law, shorn of the Hebrew–Christian tradition, these conceptions can only retain a 'mere mesmeric force' and cannot be 'inferred from anything whatever'.[16] I think Miss Anscombe would say that I have shown nothing more than this in my above arguments. What I have said about the independence of morality from religion is quite correct for this 'corrupt' age, where the basic principles of a divine-law conception of ethics appear merely as practical major premises on a par with the principle of utility and the like. In such contexts a moral 'ought' can only have a psychological force. Without God, it can have no 'discernible content' for the conception of moral obligation 'only operates in the context of law.'[17] By such moves as I have made above, I have, in effect, indicated how moral obligation *now* has only a delusive appearance of content. And in claiming that without God there still can be genuine moral obligations I have mani-

fested 'a detestable desire to retain the atmosphere of the term
"morally obligatory" where the term itself no longer has a
genuine use.'[18] 'Only if we believe in God as a law-giver can
we come to believe that there is anything a man is categorically bound to do on pain of being a bad man.'[19] The concept
of obligation has, without God, become a Holmesless Watson.
In our present context, Miss Anscombe argues, we should, if
'psychologically possible', jettison the concepts of moral
obligation, moral duty and the like and approach ethics only
after we have developed a philosophical psychology which
will enable us to clarify what pleasure is, what a human
action is and what constitutes human virtue and a distinctively
'human flourishing'.[20]

I shall not be concerned here with the larger issues raised by
Miss Anscombe's paradoxical, excessively obscure, yet
strangely challenging remarks. I agree, of course, that
philosophical psychology is important, but I am not convinced that we have not 'done' ethics and cannot profit-
ably 'do' ethics without such a philosophical psychology.
I shall, however, be concerned here only to point out that
Miss Anscombe has not shown us that the notion of moral
obligation is unintelligible or vacuous without God and his
laws.

We have already seen that if so-and-so is called a divine
command or an ordinance of God, then it is obviously something that the person who believes it to be a divine command
or ordinance of God will believe he ought to obey, for he
would not call anything a *divine* command or an ordinance
of *God* unless he thought he ought to obey it. But we ourselves, by our own moral insight, must judge that such commands or promulgations are worthy of such an appellation.
Yet no moral conceptions follow from a command or law as
such. And this would be true at any time whatsoever. It is a
logical and not a historical consideration.

Now it is true that if you believe in God in such a way as to accept God as your Lord and Master, and if you believe that something is an ordinance of God, then you ought to try to follow this ordinance. But if you behave like this it is not because you base morals on religion or on a law concept of morality, but because he who can bring himself to say 'my God' uses 'God' and cognate words evaluatively. To use such an expression is already to make a moral evaluation; the man expresses a decision that he is morally bound to do whatever God commands. 'I ought to do whatever this Z commands' is an expression of moral obligation. To believe in God, as we have already seen, involves the making of a certain value judgment; that is to say, the believer believes that there is a Z such that Z is worthy of worship. But his value judgment cannot be derived from just examining Z, or from hearing Z's commands or laws. Without a pro-attitude on the part of the believer toward Z, without a decision by the individual concerned that Z is worthy of worship, nothing or moral kind follows. But no decision of this sort is entailed by discoveries about Z or by finding out what Z commands or wishes. It is finally up to the individual to decide that this Z is worthy of worship, that this Z ought to be worshipped, that this Z ought to be called his Lord and Master. We have here a moral use of 'ought' that is logically prior to any law conception of ethics. The command gains obligatory force because it is judged worthy of obedience. If someone says, 'I do not pretend to appraise God's laws, I just simply accept them because God tells me to', similar considerations obtain. This person judges that there is a Z that is a proper object of obedience. This expresses his own moral judgment, his own sense of what he is obliged to do.

A religious belief depends for its viability on our sense of good and bad—our own sense of worth—and not vice versa. It is crucial to an understanding of morality that this truth about the uses of our language be understood. Morality cannot be based on religion and I (like Findlay) would even go

so far as to deny in the name of morality that any Z whatsoever could be an object or being worthy of worship. But
whether or not I am correct in this last judgment, it remains
the case that each person with his own finite and fallible
moral awareness must make decisions of this sort for himself. This would be so whether he was in a Hebrew–Christian
tradition or in a 'corrupt' and 'shallow' consequentialist
tradition or in any tradition whatsoever. A moral understanding must be logically prior to any religious assent.

NOTES

[1] Brunner, Emil (1947), *The Divine Imperative*, translated by Olive Wyon,
London: Lutterworth Press, chapter IX

[2] Nowell-Smith, P. H. (1966), 'Morality: Religious and Secular' in Ramsey
Ian (ed), *Christian Ethics and Contemporary Philosophy*, London: SCM Press

[3] Ewing, A. C. (1961), 'The Autonomy of Ethics' in Ramsey, Ian (ed)
Prospect for Metaphysics, London: Allen and Unwin

[4] ibid., p 39   [5] ibid., p 40   [6] ibid., p 4.

[7] See Rees, D. A. (1961), 'Metaphysical Schemes and Moral Principles' in
Prospect for Metaphysics, op. cit., p 23

[8] Hepburn, Ronald (1958), *Christianity and Paradox*, London: C. A. Watts,
p 132

[9] This is surely to assume a lot.

[10] Finally we must be quite clear that X's being good is but a necessary
condition for X's being the perfect good. But what would be a sufficient
condition? Do we really know? I think we do not. We do not know how to
identify the referent of 'the Perfect Good'. Thus in one clear sense we do not
understand what such a phrase means.

[11] This objection has been made in an unpublished paper by Professor T. P.
Brown.

[12] Findlay, J. N. (1955), 'Can God's Existence be Disproved?' in Antony
Flew and Alasdair MacIntyre (eds), *New Essays in Philosophical Theology*, New
York: Macmillan Company, pp 47–56

[13] Russell, Bertrand and Copleston, F. C. (1957), 'The Existence of God: A
Debate' in Bertrand Russell, *Why I am not a Christian*, London: Allen and
Unwin, pp 145–7

[14] Anscombe, Elizabeth (January 1958), 'Modern Moral Philosophy' in
Philosophy, vol. 33, no. 8

[15] ibid., p 5   [18] ibid., p 18
[16] ibid., p 8   [19] ibid., p 6
[17] ibid., p 18   [20] ibid., pp 1, 15, 18

TWO

RELIGIOUS VERSUS SECULAR MORALITY

I

IN CHAPTER ONE, I attempted to develop and defend what is, in essentials, an argument first set forth by Plato in his *Euthyphro*. It is an argument designed to establish that a morality, even a religious morality, cannot simply be based on a belief in God. That God ordains or wills certain things cannot be the ultimate ground for our moral assent.

It may be prudent to do what a powerful being—a Hitler or a Stalin, for example—commands, but this certainly does not make the doing of it morally obligatory. It does not by itself even constitute a relevant moral reason for doing it. For 'God commanded it' to be a morally relevant reason for doing something, let alone a definitive moral reason for doing it, it must, at least, be the case that God is good. A believer, of course, believes this to be the case, but what grounds does he have for this belief? If he says that he knows this to be true because the record of the Bible, the state of the world or the behaviour of Jesus displays God's goodness, the believer himself clearly displays by his very response that he has some logically prior criterion for moral belief that is not based on the fact that there is a deity.

Yet it is more natural for a believer to reject the very question 'How do you know God is good?' on the grounds that it is a senseless question. It is like asking 'How do you know that scarlet things are red?' or 'How do you know that puppies are young?' If he is something of a philosopher, he might tell you that ' "God is good", like "puppies are young", is analytic, it is a truth of language. We could not—logically could not—call any being, ground of being, power or force "God" if we were not also prepared to attribute or ascribe goodness to it.' This is indeed so. As we can only call the dog we see in the park a puppy, if we already understand 'young' and know how to judge whether or not a dog is young, so we can properly call some being, force or power 'God' only if we already understand what it is for something to be good and know how to judge whether or not such a being, force or power is good. In this fundamental way even the devout religious believer cannot possibly base his morality on his religion—that is, on his belief in God. He, too, has an even more fundamental criterion for judging something to be good or morally obligatory. Since this is so, God cannot be the only criterion for moral belief, let alone the only fundamental or adequate moral criterion. We must look elsewhere for the foundations of morality.

A defender of Judaeo-Christian ethics could accept this and still maintain that there could be no adequate or genuine morality without God. He might say that though we must have some understanding of good and we must have some criteria for moral terms which are not derived from our religion, it remains the case that only a God-centred morality could satisfy our most persistent moral demands.

How could religious moralists defend such a claim? They could start by arguing that I have considered the question of morality and religion in too rarified an atmosphere. I have treated morality as if it were in a vacuum. I have failed to take into consideration the enormous importance to morality of questions concerning man's human nature (his actual desires and needs) and the concrete nature of the world he lives in. Indeed we cannot derive what we ought to do from any statements which merely assert that so and so is the case; but in deciding what to make the case, in deciding what is worth seeking, what is ultimately desirable, we most surely need to have some clear understanding of what is the case.

Such an understanding is something to which any sane morality aspires.

Any realistic morality—secular or religious—links in some close way with what men on reflection actually desire and with that illusive thing we call human happiness. Such moralists would be in fundamental agreement with Nowell-Smith's remark that 'if men had no desires and aversions, if they felt no joy and no remorse, if they were totally indifferent to everything in the universe, there would be no such thing as choice and we should have no concept of morality, of good and evil.'[1]

We surely cannot crudely identify 'good' with 'object of desire', yet if men did not have certain desires and aversions, certain wants and needs, there would be no morality at all

Such moralists could then point out that philosophers as different as Aristotle and Mill have wanted to say something more than this: we indeed seek many things and have many desires, yet all are but particular expressions of a more general desire. A man may want a civic office, a well-heeled wife, the ownership of a newspaper, a trusteeship in a university, but he wants these things because they are means to power and prestige. He, in turn, craves power and prestige because he is seeking security. He seeks security because only through attaining security can he attain what all men desire, namely, human happiness. And it is at just this juncture that the religious moralist can attack the purely secular moralist. He will meet the secularist on his own grounds and argue that the secular moralist's great mistake *is in failing to see that in God alone can man find lasting happiness—the goal of all moral striving.*[2]

John Hick defends such a view in his essay 'Belief and Life: The Fundamental Nature of the Christian Ethic.'[3] It is also defended in a similar manner by Alasdair MacIntyre in his *Difficulties in Christian Belief.*[4] Following Aristotle and Mill, they claim that our basic desire is the desire for happiness·

it is the ultimate goal for all human beings. They recognize that to make this claim is not to assert a grand anthropological hypothesis. Hick makes it quite explicit that his statement has the status of an implicit definition. Yet he claims that this does not make the identification of the final object of human desire trivial.

Christian philosophers such as Professor Hick take yet another step with Aristotle. While not sharing Aristotle's particular conception of the content of human happiness or lasting contentment, they do share his overall semantic requirement that we identify human happiness with whatever it is that we humans desire simply for its own sake and never simply as a means to anything else. That is, they agree, that Aristotle was right in claiming that 'happiness is that which mankind desires above all else.' We seek this or that specific objective because we rightly or wrongly believe that its attainment will minister to our happiness.

The question as to what will and what will not make us happy or contribute to our happiness is a factual question. The correct answer will depend on what men are like and how the world goes. Aristotle (as well as Plato) thought that the happiness of any kind of creature consisted in the fulfilment of its own *telos* or purpose, that is, in the realization of its own end. The happiness of a human being must accordingly consist in the fulfilment of what it is that makes a man a man. In Cardinal Mercier's phrase, it consists in the achievement of 'man's rational nature'. If we realize our distinctively human potentialities, we will attain happiness; if not, we will not.

If we have a firm faith in God, these religious moralists argue, and if we have some understanding of what he wishes for us, we can come to see that man's purpose is very different from what a man with secular knowledge alone would take to be man's purpose. In fact, in a very real sense, God is the sustainer or custodian of our values, for without him, our lives would have no purpose. Even if 'good' cannot be defined as 'what God wills', knowledge of the reality revealed in the Jewish and Christian creeds makes it plain that man lives not for himself alone but was created by God for fellowship with Him. Man's purpose involves the love and acknowledgment of God. To love God is the fundamental reason for man's existence. If the fulfilling of one's nature is in harmony with the determining realities of one's total environment, such a fulfilment will bring happiness. If we accept the creeds of Judaism and Christianity, we believe that the 'divine purpose of man is destined to final fruition'. We *trust* that the universe is not such as to finally frustrate man's efforts to fulfil his purpose and to attain not only happiness but eternal bliss. If we come to know God we must also come to regard him as a good shepherd who will protect his children and guide their lives according to his own good purpose.

A recognition of this fact about our world will free man from anxiety. Our attitude toward life will, in some significant respects, be like the attitude of a very small child whose parents unambivalently love him. The child's sense of being securely loved is a major psychological device in giving him a sense of peace, warmth and stability. Similarly, 'the knight of faith' will, Hick argues, manifest the 'fruit of the spirit' which is 'love, joy, peace, patience, kindness, goodness, faithfulness, gentleness, self-control'. If our faith could be like a child's, we could live with this inner contentment and give uncalculatingly to others; but Hick, like Niebuhr, is aware that since 'the fall' the ambivalent, tortured creature we call 'the human animal' cannot attain this blissful state. Nonetheless, he can sometimes approximate it, and the closer he comes to this, the closer he comes to attaining genuine happiness.

II

However, it is on these very contested grounds concerning human happiness and the ends of life that religious morality has a competitor in secular morality. Many secular moralists see that the overall rationale of moral rules is linked to achieving the maximum in human happiness and the minimum in human suffering for all the people involved. Against such a secular conception of morality, a religious moralist must make good his claim that secular moralities, like utilitarianism, lack a real understanding of what happiness is. They lack the awareness of a transcendent Divine Purpose that gives man the supreme gift of blessedness, whose full glory transcends our imaginations. As the Scottish Shorter Catechism puts it, 'Man's chief end is to glorify God and enjoy Him for ever and ever.' Man's fullest happiness, man's distinctive flourishing, consists in the attainment of this state.

It may, the religious moralist will continue, indeed be true that we cannot determine what is good or what we ought to do from a knowledge that there is a deity and that He issues certain commands. In that sense Plato is right and morality is independent of religion, but in another deeper, more important sense, morality is dependent on religion. The above remarks about happiness and man's purpose should make this 'deeper sense' reasonably clear. Understanding what morality is all about, secularists and religious people alike know that morality is integrally connected with human happiness. But the man of faith alone realizes that man, with his deep and pervasive longing for immortality, can find 'lasting and supreme happiness' only in God. As St Augustine says: 'Our hearts are restless until they find rest in Thee.' Without God, life is just one damn thing after another, without our ever knowing what we want or why we want it. Without a belief in God—a Sovereign Lord—who loves us, promises us protection and finally the bliss of immortality, our lives must remain impoverished. Inner peace and contentment can come only through a belief in God.

Secular ethics, it is argued, also links morality with human desires and needs, but the picture of human happiness it gives us is, at best, superficial. Missing the dark insights of Pascal and Kierkegaard, secular ethics exhibits no deep understanding of the innermost wishes, fears, anxieties or hopes of the human animal. But a religiously backed morality does understand that without God man's deepest wishes cannot be gratified. Without God, man will despair and will not attain the deepest, truest form of human happiness.

It is not only true that man will despair without God, but if we are aware of the reality of God, we will come to see that many of the things we would otherwise rationally desire are not really worth having. Like Hesse's Sidartha, we will undergo a radical transformation. We will come to see that many of our hopes are vain and that the possibility of realizing other deeper, more lasting, desires becomes a reality for us when we come to know the reality of God. What it is rational to do, and what constitutes a reasonable wish, depends on the environment in which we live. The recognition of the truth, or even the meaningfulness of certain creedal or doctrinal statements, makes it rational to seek certain things that it would otherwise be irrational to seek. If, for example, we accept the creedal and doctrinal statements of Christianity, the moral teachings of this religion become rational, while without the creed and the doctrine, the moral code is 'absurdly quixotic and impractical'.

In this way the Christian ethic is based on Christian beliefs about the nature of God and his relation to man. If we understand them we can understand the point of doing some things that would otherwise seem very foolish. As Niebuhr has said, the Christian ethic is not an ethic that squares with our secular understanding of what we ought to do. In accepting the Christian ethic or, for that matter, any religious ethic, we are not just accepting a set of commands; beyond that we are freely adopting a way of life that will radically transform our aims in life. And the way of life depicted in Jesus' teachings directs us voluntarily to relinquish much that we would ordinarily prize. We are asked to give up wealth, power and the approval of one's peers. Christian morality, as any religious morality, is a way of life that aims, in general, not at promoting the agent's own interests, as these are usually identified, but rather at serving his neighbours in their various needs. While it need not be an ascetic or 'world-renouncing' ethic, the Christian ethic is a markedly other-regarding ethic. It requires sacrifices of human beings and it requires them to put aside what, from a purely secular point of view, they would take to be in their own rational interest. But it also claims that human beings will only achieve lasting human happiness if they so act.

God supplies us with the motive for acting in what, from a secular point of view, seems to be a very odd way. It is Professor Hick's contention that once we come to really know God, once we come to know what he is like and why he has created us, then we will freely decide to live in a way radically different from the one we would choose if we did not know our redeemer. In fact, if we really know God, we must love him. 'Knowing' here is not just an acquaintance with a certain experience or the acknowledgment that a certain statement is true: to know 'God as Lord and Father is to live in a certain way, which is determined by the character and purposes of God'.[5] To be aware of God is to see the world from a different slant and to react differently to it. (That does not mean that such awareness is only to see the world from such a slant.) Given this specifically religious awareness, many policies and aims that would otherwise be unreasonable become highly reasonable and desirable aims or policies. Given a proper understanding of the nature of reality the seemingly unpractical nature of the Christian and Jewish codes will now be seen to be highly practical—indeed they square with what a rational man would desire. Given such a new understanding of the world, we see what genuine happiness is and how it is utterly dependent on God. As Hick puts it:[6]

> Jesus' teaching does not command that we live in a way which runs counter to our deepest desires, and which would thus require some extraordinary counterbalancing inducement. Rather, he reveals to us the true nature of the world in which we are living and indicates in the light of this the only way in which our deepest desires can be fulfilled. In an important sense, then, Jesus does not propose any new motive for action. He does not set up a new end to be sought, or provide a new impulse to seek an already familiar end. Instead, he offers a new vision, or mode of appreciation of the world, such that to live humanely in the world as it is thus seen to be, is to live the kind of life which Jesus describes. The various attitudes and policies for living which he sought to replace are expressions of a sense of insecurity which is natural enough if the world really is, as most people take it to be, an arena of competing interests in which each must safeguard himself and his own against the rival egoisms of his neighbours. If human life is essentially a form of animal life, and human civilization a refined jungle in which self-concern operates more subtly but not less surely than by animal tooth and claw, then the quest for invulnerability in its many guises is entirely rational. To seek security in the form of power over others, whether physical, psychological, economic, or political, or in the form of recognition and acclaim would then be indicated by the character of our environment. But Jesus rejects these attitudes and objectives as based upon an estimate of the world which is false because it is atheistic; it assumes that there is no God, or at least none such as Jesus knew. Jesus was accordingly far from being an idealist, if by this we mean one who sets up ideals and recommends us to be guided by them instead of by the realities around us. He was a realist presenting a life in which the neighbour is valued equally with the self as indicated by the character of the universe as it really is. He urged men to live in terms of reality; and his morality differs from the normal morality of the world because his view of reality differs from the normal view of the world . . . The universe is so constituted that to live in it in the manner which Jesus has described is to build one's life upon enduring foundations, whilst to live in the opposite way is to go 'against the grain' of things and to court ultimate disaster. Jesus assumes that as rational beings we want to live in terms of reality, and he is concerned to tell us what the true structure of reality is.

III

What are we to say to Hick? One thing is quite plain—and here I am in agreement with Professor Hick: if the creedal and doctrinal claims of Judaism or Christianity were true, then it would indeed be rational to act as Hick's believer is convinced we ought to act. We cannot deduce moral statements from factual ones but we all repeatedly and typically use factual statements to back up our moral statements. The effects of air pollution on health and of population growth on the environment are clearly relevant to the choices human beings should make about technological development and population growth. That Jones habitually has several lovers and regularly drinks himself into a stupor is patently relevant to Frannie's decision that she ought not to marry him. A person who knowingly ignores such factual considerations in making moral decisions behaves irrationally. A 'knight of the absurd' who utterly ignores the relevant facts in coming to moral decisions is a man who clearly belongs in an insane asylum.

So far, I agree with Hick. We should make our moral judgments in the light of what the facts are. But it is just Hick's account of the facts that seems to me to be so totally unrealistic, so devoid of a genuine sense of reality. In critically considering his account, all the old, as well as some new, objections to religion come trouping back in. We have no evidence at all for believing in the existence or love of God. None of the proofs works; we (or some of us, at any rate) have religious experiences, but these religious experiences do not establish, even with any probability, that there is an unlimited being, a transcendent cause of the universe. These experiences can always be interpreted naturalistically or non-theistically. There is no logical bridge from these experiences to God.[7] Worse still, the very meaning of the term God is opaque. We say 'God is distinct from the universe and the creator of the universe', but we have no idea of what we would have to encounter now or hereafter to encounter a transcendent cause or a creator of the universe. If we speak, as Father Bochenski has,[8] of 'supernatural perceptions', we are (to put it mildly) 'explaining' the obscure by the still more obscure. The plain fact is that we do not have any grounds for believing that God exists or for believing that his purposes are good; and our troubles are compounded when we realize that we do not even know what we would have to experience for it to be true or even probable that God exists, or that God loves man. That this is so raises, as Professor Hick is keenly aware, serious questions about the very intelligibility of such utterances. It will do no good to say 'We now see as through a darkened glass but hereafter we shall see face-to-face', for, even if man is immortal, if we do not now know what it would be like to verify the statements 'God exists' and 'God loves us', the simple fact that we some day may wake up on 'the other shore' will not help us to verify that there is a God. Immortality is possible even in a Godless universe.

Hick, as part of a good Protestant tradition, might welcome such an answer by saying that unless we are in 'the circle of faith', we cannot even understand these matters. But this reply will not do, for while we might take it on faith that God exists, in lieu of having evidence for his existence, we cannot take the intelligibility of 'God exists' or 'God shall raise the quick and the dead' utterly on faith, for we must first understand _what_ it is we are to take on faith.[9] But even if we were able to appeal to faith here, we are still faced with the quite elementary and yet quite staggering anthropological fact that there are thousands of religions with conflicting revelations, most of them claiming ultimate authority and ultimate truth in matters of religion. Which one are we to choose? Why should we think, as finite men, historically and ethnically bound, that our religion and our tribe alone should have the one true revelation? We are members of one historically bound culture on a minor planet in an unbelievably vast universe. Why should it be that in these matters we have a unique hold on the truth? To think that we do is to have a fantastically unrealistic picture of the world.

If we say, by way of rebuttal, that in talking about religion we should only consider the great or the higher religions, we run into a host of difficulties. First, these religions often differ very radically from each other. Consider, for example, Judaism and Thervada Buddhism. Furthermore, the laudatory labels 'great' and 'higher' are question-begging. Do we decide they are higher by an appeal to our own faith or our own revelation? If we do, we move in a very small and vicious circle. Do we decide they are higher or great religions because they have more members or cover geographically wider areas? If we do, why should such considerations be taken as relevant reasons for such a judgment? Certainly we do not use such criteria in judging which cultures have the most advanced forms of music, dance or science. Such an appeal in religion is quite arbitrary. If we say that we call these religions higher because they exhibit a deeper moral insight into man's condition, then we have used—as I think we often do in practice—our own quite secular moral understanding to judge religions and we clearly indicate that we do not need these religions to back up our morality. (Viewed in this way, Christianity and Judaism do not seem to me to come off as spectacular successes.)

In short, there is not the slightest reason to believe that the Christian is living according to 'the reality principle' while the non-Christian, and the secularist in particular, are deluded about man's true estate. Christianity is myth-eaten. The very intelligibility of the key concepts of the religion is seriously in question; there is no evidence whatsoever for the existence of God; and when we keep an anthropological perspective in mind, we will come to recognize that the revelation and authority of Christianity are but one revelation and one authority among thousands of conflicting revelations and authorities. Given this state of affairs, it is the epitome of self-delusion to believe that Jesus really reveals what the true structure of reality is

IV

Those in the tradition of Kierkegaard are likely to assert here that I have missed the deepest appeal of Christianity. Certainly God, Christ and religion in general are absurd; Christianity is surely a genuine scandal to the intellect, but we need it all the same, for, as Camus and Sartre recognize, man's very condition in this world is absurd and if there is no God, man's life must be meaningless—a stupid game of charades, without any rationale at all. It is true, as Luther said, that if a man is to be a sound-believing Christian, he must tear out the eyes of his reason, but unless he does this, unless—indeed in utter darkness—he makes the leap of faith, he will never attain lasting happiness. Without a belief in God, he will be driven to despair. This is so because man can only find lasting happiness in God. This is why, in spite of all the intellectual and emotional impediments to belief, one should join the circle of faith.

In all sobriety, what we need to ask is this: is there good sociological or psychological evidence to show that people will despair, will lose their sense of identity and purpose if they do not become followers of Christ? There are cultures, cultures that have never even heard of Christianity, let alone adopted it, that have, as far as we can tell, members who are just as happy and live with just as much a sense of purpose as we do. This shows that it is not true that we can save ourselves from despair only by following Christ. The burden of proof is surely on the Christian to show that the Christian faith alone saves man from despair and gives orientation and point to his life.

Perhaps what is being claimed is the more general thesis that without a belief in God, man will be driven to despair. Neither Judaism nor Christianity need be taken to be essential. But belief in divine providence is essential.

However, while it is true that there are people whose lives

would lose all direction if they lost their God, it is also true that there are non-believers who have lived happy and productive lives, people such as John Dewey, George Eliot and George Bernard Shaw. To this it is natural to reply: 'Well, that may work for intellectuals, for some severely reflective men who will not draw warmth from the tribal campfire, but it will never work for the plain man.' But it has. Chinese civilization, for example, or that part of it under the sway of Confucianism, has a religion which, for all practical purposes, is Godless, yet Confucianists have continued to live purposeful lives.

It is interesting to note that when such arguments for the necessity of faith are made by religious apologists, they do not, as a rule, put such a contention to empirical test, but assert, after the fashion of Kierkegaard, that a man *must* despair without God. The non-believer who does not show despair is really a man who suffers from some 'hidden perturbation'—some deep but disguised estrangement from his true being. While this may be true of some non-believers, it remains for the believer to show that there is in all non-believers some such disquietude. (They might start by considering the lives of Bentham, Freud and Dewey.) We need evidence here and not just *a priori dicta* that man must despair without God or that man will be happier with a belief in God. Moreover, it should be shown that man needs not just an undifferentiated theism, but also the concrete specifications of a living theistic religion. Thus we are led back to Judaism and Christianity.

Pascal shows in his *Pensées* that with Christ man has the hope of redemption and eternal bliss that the secularist does not have; but with the Jewish and Christian religions, one also has a sense of sin and unworthiness that, as in the case of Stephan Dædalus in *The Portrait of The Artist as a Young Man*, or Jerome in *La Porte Etroite*, can drive one to self-loathing and despair. If it is replied that since The Fall we have been tormented and that the 'old Adam' is in us all—even after Christ came to redeem us—then what grounds have we for claiming that people within Christianity will be happier than people outside the 'circle of faith'?

Generally speaking, believers are neither happier nor are they better adjusted than non-believers. There are sick, paranoid and vile believers and there are sick, paranoid and vile non-believers; there are sane, humane and happy believers, and there are sane, humane and happy non-believers. Personal virtue and vice seem to be completely independent of doctrinal affiliation.

Not many (if any) religious apologists wish to make this issue an empirical, anthropological issue. They have a certain picture of life, and reasoning in accordance with this picture they conclude that man must despair without God. Secular moralists, they argue, can have no real understanding of what human happiness is. Here we have a purely *a priori* philosophical argument. But is it a good one? I think not. In the first place, the religionist frequently depicts a secularist morality in a way—as Hick does—that makes it seem egoistic and a kind of gross hedonism in which man is nothing more than a purely self-concerned, clever little animal.[10] We come to picture secular moralities as committing us to a vision of the good life that consists in devotion to pleasures like those gained from taking Turkish baths and watching belly dancers. But no secularist need deny the dignity of man nor devote himself exclusively, or at all, to such pleasures. Once we rid ourselves of such stereotypes, why should we say that the believer alone knows what 'true happiness' is?

At this point, Hick and other theologians, both Protestant and Catholic, trot out a very ancient argument—an argument that in essence goes back to Plato and Aristotle. The happiness of a human being must consist in the fulfilment of what it is that makes a man a man. Only when he achieves what it is that he was 'cut out to be' will he achieve lasting contentment. But the believer alone knows what man was cut out to be, so he alone can know the nature of true happiness and thus of true virtue. (That is a slippery 'thus' but we shall let it pass.)

But why should we assume that man was cut out to be anything, that he has some function that he must realize if he is not to suffer alienation? Man has certain distinctive capabilities: he can reason, that is, he can use symbols; he is permanently sexed; he alone laughs; he is the only animal to suffer anxiety and fear death. But why does he realize himself more adequately by developing any or all of those capacities? Perhaps he would be happier, for example, if he were less intellectual. And how can we show that he was cut out for anything? Policemen, teachers, thieves, bar-maids, janitors and barbers have certain roles, certain more or less distinctive functions. So do husbands, suitors, fathers and daughters. All of us have diverse social roles—roles that frequently conflict. But what is our role or function *qua* human being? While firemen have a clear function, man does not. The question 'What are people for?' has no clear meaning in the way that 'What are customs officers for?' does. And to say that men were made to worship and love God is completely question-begging. It seems to me that man was not made for anything.[11]

The inevitable counter is that if man was not made for something, if there is not something he was cut out to be, human living will be a nihilistic nightmare, for man's life will then be totally without purpose or point. If God did not create man for some end there can be no purpose to human living. It is when we see this—it is just when we see and take to heart the fact that without God life would be as Hardy and Schopenhauer depict it—that we are driven to God. We will then realize, as Tolstoy came to, that without God our lives will be without a purpose, without a rationale.

V

There is a plethora of confusion in such apologetics. It is indeed true that a purposeless life is a horrible life, a life that no
sane man could tolerate. Dostoyevsky shrewdly observes in
The House of the Dead 'that if one wanted to crush, to annihilate
a man utterly, to inflict on him the most terrible of punish-
ments so that the most ferocious murderer would shudder at
it and dread it beforehand, one need only give him work of an
absolutely, completely useless and irrational character.' If a
man were condemned to pour water from one bucket to
another and then back again, day after day, year after year,
it would indeed drive him to despair. A life made up of
actions which were devoid of all rational point or intent
would be a maddening, meaningless life. But when traditional Christian philosophers talk about purpose and the
purpose of life, they are not talking about having a purpose in
that sense. They argue, as Cardinal Mercier and Professor
Hick have argued, that man is a creature of God, created by
God to worship Him, and to enter into a covenant with Him.
That is man's purpose. It is in this sense that life must have a
purpose if man is to achieve final happiness. Yet this sort of
purpose is far more esoteric and metaphysical than the purpose Dostoyevsky was talking about. Religious moralists
assume, as we have seen, that man has an essence or a *telos*—
a purpose which he will realize if and only if he becomes what
he was cut out by his Creator to become. It is not enough
that we avoid the sort of situations Dostoyevsky alludes to,
but we must fulfil our essence as well, for without this we will
remain alienated and estranged.

But, as we have seen, this makes the groundless and perhaps even senseless assumption that man has a *telos* or an
essence and that he will be happy when, and only when, he
achieves it. Furthermore, the claim that man's life will lack
purpose without God trades on a crucial ambiguity about

'purpose'. When it is claimed that without God life would have no purpose, the religious apologist is talking about a purpose for man *qua* man. He is trying to talk about man *qua* man having a purpose in the sense that an artifact, plumber, merchant, doctor or policeman has a purpose. But it is far from clear that man has a purpose in that sense. It is also entirely unclear that man must remain estranged, sensing to the full that his lot in the world is absurd, if he does not have such a purpose.

Many people feel that if man were not made for a purpose, his life must be without purpose. But here a spiritual malaise is being engendered by a conceptual confusion. Sometimes 'purpose' is used to mean function or role; but sometimes 'purpose' is used to indicate that an action was deliberately or intentionally done, that it was the carrying out of someone's aim or wish.

The second use of 'purpose'—the use that Dostoyevsky was talking about in our initial example—is such that we would say that only people and perhaps some animals could have it. When we use 'purpose' in this sense, we are speaking of people's goals, aims, intentions, motives and the like. 'Purpose' has this sense when we speak of our purpose in doing something specific: 'What was your purpose in bringing home that dog?' and 'I wonder what his purpose was in coming here?' Now this is one major way in which 'purpose' is used in which the theist and non-theist alike are in complete accord that there is purpose in our lives—God or no God. And it is true that a life devoid of purpose in that sense would, without doubt, be a dreadful, senseless affair.

By contrast, we use 'purpose' in the first sense when we ask: 'What is the purpose of that gadget in the kitchen?' or 'What is the purpose of that fence along the road?' Here we imply 'that someone did something, in the doing of which he had some purpose; namely, to bring about the thing with the purpose. Of course, *his* purpose is not identical with *its* purpose.'[12] If we accept a scientific world picture and reject a theistic world picture, we are indeed forced to say that in this first sense life is purposeless. But it is completely contrary to the truth to say that a rejection of the theistic world view robs our lives of purpose in the second sense of 'purpose'. On the contrary, one could well claim, as Baier does, that 'science has not only not robbed us of any purpose which we had before, but it has also furnished us with enormously greater power to achieve these purposes. Instead of praying for rain or a good harvest or offspring, we now use ice pellets, artificial manure or artificial insemination.'[13]

More importantly still, when we say 'life must have a purpose or there is no point of going on', we are usually using 'purpose' in the second sense. It is in this sense that we so desperately want life to have a purpose. But life can have a purpose in that sense in the twilight, or even in the complete absence, of the Gods. And whether or not something has or does not have a purpose in the first sense of 'purpose' does not matter at all, for having or lacking a purpose in this first sense carries neither *kudos* nor stigma. To say that a man has a purpose in this first sense is actually offensive for it involves treating man as a kind of tool or artifact. It is degrading for a man to be regarded as merely serving a purpose. If I turned to you and asked, 'What are you for?' it would be insulting to you. It would be as if I had reduced you to 'the level of a gadget, a domestic animal or perhaps a slave'.[14] I would be treating you merely as a means and not as an end. Failing to have a purpose in that sense does not at all detract from the meaningfulness of life. Many of us, at any rate, would be very disturbed and think our lives meaningless if we *did* have a purpose in this first sense.

The whole tendency to think that if there is no God and if God did not create man with a built-in design then life would be totally without worth arises from muddled thinking. People who claim that if God is dead nothing matters 'mistakenly conclude that there can be no purpose *in* life because there is no purpose *of* life; that men cannot themselves adopt and achieve purposes because man, unlike a robot or a watch-dog, is not a creature with a purpose'.[15]

VI

There is a clash between the secular moralist and the Christian moralist over what will provide lasting contentment. While this may not always cause conflict over our usual daily activities, it is the source of a deeper moral conflict over what is worth seeking and how human life should be ordered. The Christian looks on life as something in which his ultimate goal or purpose as well as his basic purposes are set by God. We are, of course, free to reject this purpose, but unfailing happiness 'is only to be found in participating in that consummation, in becoming the sort of person who is able to enter into final union with God'.[16]

The intellectually harassed, non-Neanderthal, modern Christian is sorely tempted to give these strange claims a radical reinterpretation such that in some subtle sense religion becomes what it was for Matthew Arnold, 'morality tinged with emotion'. Religion on such a reinterpretation is envis-aged as 'morality strengthened and reinforced by the imagi-nation and will'.[17] For Braithwaite, a distinguished recent exponent of this view, to speak of 'entering into final union with God'[18] amounts to an expression of intention to regard one's fellow-men in a brotherly way or to act as if all men were seeking to live together in peace and harmony. Religious utterances are generally not regarded as mysterious assertions about the nature of the universe, but as expressions of inten-tion which we associate with certain parables. We may or may not believe the parables but we must at least be willing to allow the association. Such a reinterpretation may—as Jung would say—'breathe life into these ancient symbols', giving them new vitality for modern man questing for God

But such a coating to make religion respectable eats at the very substance of religion. If we finally go the way of Braithwaite we have nothing left at all. MacIntyre rightly remarks, 'such a view in reality renounces traditional religion altogether. For it omits from religion all reference to the reality of God, to God's real creating and redemptive acts. It preserves the name of religion while believing exactly what atheists believe.'[19] If a Christian takes such a Braithwaitian turn, he will no longer have any ground at all for speaking of different expectations about life's goals; there will no longer be a ground in accordance with which a Christian moralist could set himself off from a secular moralist.

MacIntyre recognizes that both the reasonably orthodox Christian and the secularist are making claims about being, or a being, that in certain crucial respects are radically different and incompatible. The Christian, for example, trusts that there is a God who created him and who acts in the world while being 'out of' or 'beyond the world'. (Phrases like these are unintelligible to many secularists; the believer, to the contrary, will not allow that they are unintelligible, but often does assert with a certain Kierkegaardian joy and verve that they are extremely paradoxical. But, after all, what is faith without paradox?) Because of this 'fact' the Christian decides to act, to direct his life in a certain way. If he knows what he is about, he will recognize that what he is seeking is an alternative to another genuine morality that is quite independent of religion.

That there are these conflicting alternative moralities is very understandable, given the nature of religion. As we finally must just opt for belief or unbelief, so finally we must just decide whether to assent to a Christian way of life rather than to a secular one. There is no morally neutral vantage point from which we can judge and choose between these conflicting ways of life. When a Christian says that his morality is more adequate than a non-Christian's, he must rely on Christian standards of judgment. But MacIntyre would have us believe that the secular moralist is no better off here. He has no neutral haven that he can retreat to that will allow him to avoid the storm and stress of personal decision. For neither the Christian moralist nor the secularist is there a genuine safe port that will protect him from such blasts. There is no avoiding a decision when questions of conduct are at stake and there is no neutral ground from which we can decide what basic decisions we are to make. There is no morally neutral ground in accordance with which we can decide between sacred and secular principles of moral evaluation.

VII

Hick and MacIntyre have correctly indicated that, taken in its living context, Christianity (as all the historical religions) necessarily involves a way of life and a morality. The moral view inherent in Christianity sharply conflicts with secular morality (naturalism, atheism, humanism). If this moral view is deleted, the very heart of Christianity is destroyed. In that sense Christian morality is obviously not independent of the Christian religion. But even here we have an inversion of things. It is Christianity as a whole that could not exist without its distinctive morality. The moral aspect, or at least some of it, might be capable of survival without the rest of the religion. Presumably MacIntyre would say to this that Christian morality would be uprooted and lack an intelligible rationale if denied a distinctively Christian, or at least theistic, conception of the nature of things. And surely there is a very considerable warrant for such a claim. Christianity, of necessity, must have a definite moral point of view and Christian morality without Christian conceptions of man, history and the cosmos is an absurdity which no rational man, 'knight of faith' or not, ought to embrace. In this sense, Christian morality is not independent of Christianity as a whole.

This statement, however, is not in conflict with those claims for independence I developed in Chapter One. What has happened here is that there has been a confusion between two senses in which we can say morality is independent of religion. The first is the one mentioned in the last paragraph and in that sense it is false to say that all morality is independent of religion. To be a Christian is to accept a certain morality and to accept this morality involves accepting the central tenets of the Christian religion. To be a Christian in Christendom is to have certain distinctive general aims and a belief that man is a creature in God's care, created by God, with a God-given purpose. (Even here it remains the case that the Christian's varied moral claims do not follow from religious cosmological claims alone. Statements such as 'Love God with your whole heart and whole mind', 'The life of the spirit is good', 'Do not eat meat on Fridays' do not entail and are not entailed by statements like 'There must be a necessary being' or 'A transcendant being created the universe' or 'A being who created everything but Himself loves us.' Such Christian moral claims are footless, irrational moral claims without Christian belief.)

In a second and more fundamental sense, however, morality cannot be based on religion. This is the sense I discussed in Chapter One and it is the sense most philosophers have had in mind when they have asserted the autonomy of morality from religion. The sense in which any morality is and must be independent of religion is this: that from the recognition and consequent statement that there is a being that some call 'God' no moral statements whatsoever follow. More generally, no moral statements at all can be derived from religious claims about what there is. This claim is not in conflict with the first sense in which it is correct to argue, as MacIntyre has, that morality is not independent of religion. (It is important, however, to note that this first sense could never serve as our basic meaning of what it is for something to be good, just.

perfect or fair. In saying 'Jesus is morally perfect' we are not saying 'Jesus is Jesus.' In saying 'An uncreated Creator of the universe is good', we are not saying 'An uncreated Creator of the universe is an uncreated Creator of the universe.' Only if we independently understood what 'perfect' and 'good' meant could we make such claims. Our knowledge of good and evil cannot be derived from our knowledge of such a being.)

When we use the more familiar word 'God', a further complication arises. 'God' is characteristically used by believers with an evaluative force. 'God is worthy of worship', as we have seen, is characteristically used analytically, for in the contexts of Judaeo-Christian religious assent and worship we would not say of any being, 'my Lord and my God . . .' or 'God I will follow Thee' or 'God loves us and protects us' unless we believed that being to be worthy of worship. In most religious contexts, the use of the word God connotes a being worthy of worship, but in deciding that there exists a being who is worthy of worship we must of necessity use our own moral insight. Knowledge that there is such a being is not, of course, just a matter of moral insight, but it essentially involves the making of a moral judgment. MacIntyre, in fine, has confused these two senses in which we can claim that morality is or is not independent of religion. In correctly seeing that in the first sense there is not this independence, MacIntyre thought that he had shown, in the second and more fundamental sense I have distinguished, that there is no such independence. But in this last sense, it is incorrect to say that morality is dependent on religious beliefs; even Christian moral beliefs cannot be derived from them.

It is evident from MacIntyre's first paragraph that it is this second sense of independence which interests him. The intellectual issue he is interested in is precisely the one involved in this second sense in which we speak of the independence of morality from religion. MacIntyre points out that 'Christianity consists of a number of assertions about what

God is and what He has done and a number of injunctions about how we ought to live. In the New Testament, the latter are made to depend on the former.'[20] MacIntyre wishes to establish this New Testament claim against the philosophic contention that the latter cannot be derived from the former and in that sense they do not depend on but are necessarily independent of the former. But, as we have shown, from definitional statements about God and from factual assertions about what God has done, is doing or will do, there follow no injunctions about how to live. And if we allow, as one crucial moral judgment, something like 'God is a Good Shepherd who watches over His flock', this judgment cannot in turn be derived from statements definitive of Godhood or factual assertions about what God does.

In sum, I have argued in this chapter that morality and religion are, in the crucial sense specified, logically independent—that is, we cannot derive moral claims from such cosmological claims as 'God exists', 'God shall raise the quick and the dead' and 'God laid the foundations of the earth.' 'X ought to be done' or 'X is good' is never identical with or derivable from 'God wills X' or 'God created X.' It is not senseless (conceptually unintelligible) to question the will of God, though it is blasphemous. I then went on to argue, as against Professor Hick, MacIntyre and others, that a God-centred ethic has no claim to provide the most adequate criterion of moral actions because it possesses the deepest and most accurate understanding of man's condition. I argued that the claims to intelligibility and claims to truth given us by Christianity and Judaism are so scandalously weak that we have no grounds for using these religions as a basis for morality or as an answer to the 'riddle of human destiny'. Finally, I argued that there are no grounds for claiming that a man's life is without purpose if there is no God. In the only sense in which it really matters, we can and do have purposes in a Godless world.

NOTES

[1] Nowell-Smith, P. H. (1961), 'Morality: Religious and Secular' in *Rationalist Annual*, p 9

[2] To show this is one of the fundamental aims of Pascal's *Pensées*.

[3] Hick, John (1959), 'Belief and Life: The Fundamental Nature of the Christian Ethic' in *Encounter*, vol. 20, no. 4, pp 494–516

[4] MacIntyre, Alasdair (1959), *Difficulties in Christian Belief*, London: SCM, p 107. It should be noted that MacIntyre has abandoned the position adumbrated in *Difficulties in Christian Belief* and has come to adopt a view very similar to my own. See his contribution in MacIntyre, Alasdair and Ricoeur, Paul (1969), *The Religious Significance of Atheism*, New York and London: Columbia University Press.

[5] Hick (1959), op. cit., p 495

[6] ibid., pp 498–99

[7] Exactly the same considerations hold for mystical experiences.

[8] See his forceful inaugural lecture, 'Theology's Central Problem', Birmingham, 1967

[9] On this point, see Nielsen, Kai (July 1963), 'Can Faith Validate God-Talk?' in *Theology Today* vol. xx, no. 2, pp 158–173

[10] Ronald Hepburn has some very effective things to say against this argument. See Hepburn, Ronald (1958), *Christianity and Paradox*, London: C. A. Watts, pp 147–54

[11] See Baier, Kurt (1957), 'The Meaning of Life, inaugural lecture, Canberra.

[12] ibid., p 19

[13] ibid., p 20

[14] ibid.

[15] ibid.

[16] MacIntyre (1959), op. cit., p 107

[17] ibid., p 104

[18] Braithwaite, R. B. (1955), *An Empiricist's View of the Nature of Religious Belief*, London: Cambridge University Press

[19] MacIntyre (1959), op. cit., p 105

[20] ibid., p 104

THREE

HUMANISTIC ETHICS

I

THERE ARE FUNDAMENTAL DIFFICULTIES and perhaps even elements of incoherence in Christian ethics, but what can a secular moralist offer in its stead? Religious morality—and Christian morality in particular—may have its difficulties, but religious apologists argue that secular morality has still greater difficulties. It leads, they claim, to ethical scepticism, nihilism or, at best, to a pure conventionalism. Such apologists could point out that if we look at morality with the cold eye of an anthropologist we will find morality to be nothing more than the often conflicting *mores* of the various tribes spread around the globe.

If we eschew the kind of insight that religion can give us, we will have no Archimedean point in accordance with which we can decide how it is that we ought to live and die. If we look at ethics from such a purely secular point of view, we will discover that it is constituted by tribal conventions, conventions which we are free to reject if we are sufficiently free from ethnocentrism. We can continue to act in accordance with them or we can reject them and adopt a different set of conventions; but whether we act in accordance with the old conventions or forge 'new tablets', we are still acting in accordance with certain conventions. In relation to these conventions certain acts are right or wrong, reasonable or unreasonable, but we cannot justify the fundamental moral conventions themselves or the ways of life which they partially codify.

When these points are conceded, theologians are in a position to press home a powerful apologetic point: when we become keenly aware of the true nature of such conventionalism and when we become aware that there is no overarching purpose that men were destined to fulfil, the myriad purposes, the aims and goals humans create for themselves, will be seen to be inadequate. When we realize that life does not have a meaning which is there to be found, but that we human beings must by our deliberate decisions give it whatever meaning it has, we will (as Sartre so well understood) undergo estrangement and despair. We will drain our cup to its last bitter drop and feel our alienation to the full. Perhaps there are human purposes, purposes to be found in life, and we can and do have them even in a Godless world; but without God there can be no one overarching purpose, no one basic scheme of human existence in virtue of which we could find a meaning for our grubby lives. It is this overall sense of meaning that man so ardently strives for, but it is not to be found in a purely secular world-view. You secularists, a new Pascal might argue, must realize, if you really want to be clear-headed, that no purely human purposes are ultimately worth striving for. What you Humanists can give us by way of a scheme of human existence will always be a poor second-best and not what the human heart most ardently longs for.

The considerations for and against an ethics not rooted in a religion are complex and involuted; a fruitful discussion of them is difficult, for in considering the matter our passions, our anxieties, our ultimate concerns (if you will) are involved, and they tend to blur our vision, enfeeble our understanding of what exactly is at stake. But we must not forget that what is at stake here is just what kind of ultimate commitments or obligations a man could have without evading any issue, without self-deception or without delusion. I shall be concerned to display and assess, to make plain and also to weigh, some of the most crucial considerations for and against a purely secular ethic. While I shall try to make clear in an objective fashion what the central issues are, I shall also give voice to my reflective convictions on this matter. I shall try to make evident my reasons for believing that we do not need God or any religious belief to support our moral convictions. I shall do this, as I think one should in philosophy, by making apparent the dialectic of the problem, the considerations for and against, and by arguing for what I take to be their proper resolution.

II

I am aware that Crisis theologians would claim that I am being naïve, but I do not see why purposes of purely human devising are not ultimately worth striving for. There is much that we humans prize and would continue to prize even in a Godless world. Many things would remain to give our lives meaning and point even after 'the death of God'.

Take a simple example. All of us want to be happy. But in certain bitter or sceptical moods we question what happiness is or we despairingly ask ourselves whether anyone can really be happy. Is this, however, a sober, sane view of the situation? I do not think that it is. Indeed, we cannot adequately define happiness in the way that we can bachelor, but neither can we in that way define chair, wind, pain and the vast majority of words in everyday discourse. For words like bachelor, triangle or father we can specify a consistent set of properties that all the things and only the things denoted by these words have, but we cannot do this for happiness, chair, pain and the like. Yet there is no great loss here. Modern philosophical analysis has taught us that such an essentially Platonic conception of definition is unrealistic and unnecessary.[1] I may not be able to define chair in the way that I can define bachelor, but I understand the meaning of chair perfectly well. In normal circumstances, at least, I know what to sit on when someone tells me to take a chair. I may not be able to define pain, but I know what it is like to be in pain and sometimes I can know when others are in pain. Similarly, though I cannot define happiness in the same way that I can define bachelor, I know what it is like to be happy, and sometimes I can judge with considerable reliability whether others are happy or sad. Happiness is a slippery word, but it is not so slippery that we are justified in saying that nobody knows what happiness is.

A man could be said to have lived a happy life if he had found lasting sources of satisfaction in his life and if he had been able to find certain goals worth while and to achieve at least some of them. He could indeed have suffered some pain and anxiety, but his life, for the most part, must have been free from pain, estrangement and despair and must, on balance, have been a life which he has liked and found worth while. Surely we have no good grounds for saying that no one achieves such a balance or that no one is ever happy even for a time. We all have some idea of what would make us happy and of what would make us unhappy; many people, at least, can remain happy even after 'the death of God'. At any rate, we need not strike Pascalian attitudes, for even in a purely secular world there are permanent sources of human happiness for anyone to avail himself of.

What are these relatively permanent sources of human happiness that we all want or need? What is it which, if we have it, will give us the basis for a life that could properly be said to be happy? We all desire to be free from pain and want. [Even masochists do not seek pain for its own sake; they endure pain because this is the only psychologically acceptable way of achieving something else (usually sexual satisfaction) that is so gratifying to them that they will put up with the pain to achieve it.] We all want a life in which sometimes we can enjoy ourselves and in which we can attain our fair share of some of the simple pleasures that we all desire. They are not everything in life, but they are important, and our lives would be impoverished without them.

We also need security and emotional peace. We need and want a life in which we will not be constantly threatened with physical or emotional harassment. Again, this is not the only thing worth seeking, but it is an essential ingredient in any adequate picture of the good life.

Human love and companionship are also central to a happy life. We prize them and a life which is without them is most surely an impoverished life, a life that no man, if he would take the matter to heart, would desire. But I would most emphatically assert that human love and companionship are quite possible in a Godless world, and the fact that life will some day inexorably come to an end and cut off love and companionship altogether enhances rather than diminishes their present value.

Furthermore, we all need some sort of creative employment or meaningful work to give our lives point, to save them from boredom, drudgery and futility. A man who can find no way to use the talents he has, or a man who can find no work which is meaningful to him, will indeed be a miserable man. But again there is work—whether it be as a surgeon, a farmer or a fisherman—that has a rationale even in a world without God. And poetry, music and art retain their beauty and enrich our lives even in the complete absence of God or the gods.

We want and need art, music and the dance. We find pleasure in travel and conversation and in a rich variety of experiences. The sources of human enjoyment are obviously too numerous to detail, but all of them are achievable in a Godless universe. If some can be ours, we can attain a reasonable measure of happiness. Only a Steppenwolfish personality, beguiled by impossible expectations and warped by irrational guilts and fears, can fail to find happiness in the realization of such ends. But to be free of impossible expectations people must clearly recognize that there is no 'one big thing' (or, for that matter, 'one small thing') which would make them permanently happy; almost anything permanently and exclusively pursued will lead to that nausea that Sartre has so forcefully brought to our attention. But we can, if we are not too sick and if our situation is not too precarious, find lasting sources of human happiness in a purely secular world.

It is not only happiness for ourselves that can give us something of value, but there is the need to do what we can to diminish the awful sum of human misery in the world. I have never understood those who say that they find contemporary life meaningless because they find nothing worthy of devoting their energies to. Throughout the world there is an immense amount of human suffering, suffering that can be partially alleviated through a variety of human efforts. Why can we not find a meaningful life in devoting ourselves, as did Doctor Rieux in Albert Camus *La Peste*, to relieving somewhat the sum total of human suffering? Why cannot this give our lives point and an overall rationale? It is childish to think that by human effort we will some day totally rid the world of suffering and hate, of deprivation and sadness; they are a permanent feature of the human condition. But specific instances of human suffering can be alleviated. The plague is always potentially with us, but we can destroy the Nazis and we can fight for racial and social equality throughout the world. And as isolated people, as individuals in a mass society, we find people turning to us in dire need, in suffering and in emotional deprivation, and we can as individuals respond to those people and alleviate or at least acknowledge that suffering and deprivation. A man who says, 'If God is dead, nothing matters', is a spoilt child who has never looked at his fellow-man with compassion.

Yet, it might be objected, if we abandon a Judaeo-Christian *Weltanschauung*, there can, in a secular world, be no 'one big thing' to give our lives an overall rationale. We will not be able to see written in the stars the final significance of human effort. There will be no architectonic purpose to give our lives such a rationale. Like Tolstoy's Pierre in *War and Peace*, we desire somehow to gather the sorry scheme of things entire into one intelligible explanation so that we can finally crack the riddle of human destiny. We long to understand why it is that men suffer and die. If it is a factual answer that is wanted when such a question is asked, the answer is evident enough: ask any physician. But clearly that is no answer to people who seek such a general account of human existence. They want some justification for suffering; they want some way of showing that suffering is after all for a good purpose. It can, of course, be argued that suffering sometimes is a good thing, for it occasionally gives us insight and at times even brings about in the man who suffers an increased capacity to love and to be kind. But there is plainly an excessive amount of human suffering—the suffering of children in hospitals, the suffering of people devoured by cancer and the sufferings of millions of Jews under the Nazis—for which there simply is no justification. Neither the religious man nor the secularist can explain, that is, justify, such suffering and find some overall scheme of life in which it has some place, but only the religious man needs to do so. The secularist understands that suffering is not something to be justified but simply to be struggled against with courage and dignity. And in this fight, even the man who has been deprived of that which could give him some measure of happiness can still find or make for himself a meaningful human existence.

III

I have argued that purely human purposes—those goals we set for ourselves, the intentions we form—are enough to give meaning to our lives.[2] We desire happiness and we can find, even in a purely secular world, abundant sources of it. Beyond this we can find a rationale for seeking to mitigate the awful burden of human suffering. These two considerations are enough to make life meaningful. But it might be objected that I have put far too great a stress on the value of human happiness; that there are other considerations in life, other values that are intrinsically worthwhile. We desire self-consciousness and some sense of self-identity as well as happiness. And we do not desire them for the enjoyment and happiness that will come from them but for their own sakes.

I am inclined to agree that this is so; human happiness and the desire to avoid suffering are central but are not the only facets of morality. To acknowledge this, however, only complicates the secular picture of morality: it gives us no reason to bring in theistic concepts. I admire human beings who are non-evasive and who have a sense of their own identity, and I regard an understanding of myself as something which is to be prized for its own sake. I do not need a deity to support this appreciation or give it value.

Philosophers, and some theologians as well, might challenge what I have said in a slightly different way. It could be said that even if we add consciousness as another intrinsic good, there is not the close connection between happiness and self-awareness on the one hand and virtue or moral good on the other that I have claimed there is. That men do seek happiness as an end is one thing; that they ought to seek it as an end is another. As G. E. Moore has in effect shown,[3] we cannot derive 'X is good' from 'people desire X' or from 'X makes people happy', for it is always meaningful to ask whether or not happiness is good and whether or not we ought to seek it for its own sake. It will be argued that I, like all secularists, have confused factual and moral issues. An 'ought' cannot be derived from an 'is'; we cannot deduce that something is good from a discovery that it will make people happy. My hypothetical critic could well go on to claim that we first must justify the fundamental claim that happiness is good. Do we really have any reason to believe that happiness is good? Is the secularist in any more of a position to justify his claim than is the religionist to justify his claim that whatever God wills is good?

I would first like to point out that I have not confused factual and moral issues. One of the basic reasons I have for rejecting either a natural-law ethics or an ethics of divine commands is that both systematically confuse factual and moral issues We cannot deduce that people ought to do something from discovering that they do it or seek it; nor can we conclude from the proposition that a being exists whom people call God that we ought to do whatever that being commands In both cases we unjustifiably pass from a factual premise to a moral conclusion. Moral statements are not factual statements about what people seek or avoid, or about what a deity commands. But we do justify moral claims by an appeal to factual claims, and there is a close connection between what human beings desire on reflection and what they deem to be good. 'X is good' does not mean 'X makes for happiness', but in deciding that something is good, it is crucial to know what makes human beings happy. Both the Christian moralist and the secular moralist lay stress on human happiness. The Christian moralist—St Augustine and Pascal are perfect examples—argues that only the Christian has a clear insight into what human happiness really is and that there is no genuine happiness without God. But, as I argued in Chapter Two, we have no valid grounds for believing that only in God can we find happiness and that there are no stable sources of human happiness apart from God.

I cannot prove that happiness is good, but Christian and non-Christian alike take it in practice to be a very fundamental good. I can only appeal to your sense of psychological realism to persuade you to admit intellectually what in practice you acknowledge, namely, that happiness is good and that pointless suffering is bad. If you will acknowledge this, you must accept that I have shown that man can attain happiness even in a world without God.

Suppose some Dostoyevskian 'underground man' does not care a fig about happiness. Suppose he does not even care about the sufferings of others. How, then, can you show him to be wrong? But suppose a man does not care about God or about doing what He commands either. How can you show that such an indifference to God is wrong? If we ask such abstract questions, we can see a crucial feature about the nature of morality. Sometimes a moral agent may reach a point at which he can give no further justification for his claims but must simply, by his own deliberate decision, resolve to take a certain position. Here the claims of the existentialists have a genuine relevance. We come to recognize that, in the last analysis, nothing can take the place of a decision or resolution. In the end, we must simply decide. This recognition may arouse our anxieties and stimulate rationalization, but the necessity of making a decision is inherent in the logic of the situation. Actually, the religious moralist is in a worse position than the secularist, for he not only needs to subscribe to the principle that human happiness is good and that pain and suffering have no intrinsic value; he must also subscribe to the *outré* claims that only in God can man find happiness and that one ought to do whatever it is that God commands. 'Man can find lasting happiness only if he turns humbly to his Saviour' has the look of a factual statement and is a statement that most assuredly calls for some kind of rational support. It is not something we must or can simply decide about. But the assertion that one ought to do what is commanded by God, like the assertion that happiness is good, does appear simply to call for a decision for or against. But what it is that one is deciding for when one 'decides for God or for Christ' is so obscure as to be scarcely intelligible. Furthermore, the man who subscribes to that religious principle must subscribe to the secular claim as well. But why subscribe to this obscure second principle when there is no evidence at all for the claim that man can find happiness only in God?

Morality is not science. Moral claims direct our actions; they tell us how we ought to act; they do not simply describe what we seek or explain our preferential behaviour.[4] A secular morality need not view morality as a science or as an activity

c

that is simply descriptive or explanatory. It can and should remain a normative activity. Secular morality starts with the assumption that happiness and self-awareness are fundamental human goods and that pain and suffering are never desirable in themselves. It may finally be impossible to prove that this is so, but if people will be honest with themselves they will see that in their behaviour they clearly show that they subscribe to such a principle; and a philosopher can demonstrate that criticisms of such moral principles rest on confusions. Finally, I have tried to show that a man with secular knowledge alone can find clear and permanent sources of happiness such that whoever will avail himself of these sources of happiness can, if he is fortunate, lead a happy and purposeful life.

IV

The dialectic of our problem has not ended. The religious moralist might acknowledge that human happiness is indeed plainly a good thing while contending that secular morality, where it is consistent and reflective, will inevitably lead to some variety of egoism. An individual who recognized the value of happiness and self-consciousness might, if he were free of religious restraints, ask himself why he should be concerned with the happiness and self-awareness of others, except where their happiness and self-awareness would contribute to his own good. We must face the fact that sometimes, as the world goes, people's interests clash. Sometimes the common good is served only at the expense of some individual's interests. An individual must therefore, in such a circumstance, sacrifice what will make him happy for the common good. Morality requires this sacrifice of us, when it is necessary for the common good; morality, any morality, exists in part at least to adjudicate between the conflicting interests and demands of people. It is plainly evident that everyone cannot be happy all the time and that sometimes one person's happiness or the happiness of a group is at the expense of another person's happiness.

Morality requires that we attempt to distribute happiness as evenly as possible. We must be fair: each person is to count for one and none is to count for more than one. Whether we like a person or not, whether he is useful to his society or not, his interests and what will make him happy, must be considered in any final decision as to what ought to be done. The requirements of justice make it necessary that each person be given equal consideration. I cannot justify my neglect of another person in some matter of morality simply on the grounds that I do not like him, that he is not a member of my set or that he is not a productive member of society. The religious apologist will argue that behind these requirements of justice as fairness there lurks the ancient religious principle that men are creatures of God, each with an infinite worth, and that men are never to be treated only as means but as persons deserving of respect in their own right. They have an infinite worth simply as persons.

My religious critic, following out the dialectic of the problem, should query why you should respect someone, why you should treat all people equally, if doing this is not in your interest or not in the interests of your group. No purely secular justification can be given for so behaving. My critic now serves his *coup de grâce*: the secularist, as does the 'knight of faith', acknowledges that the principle of respect for persons is a precious one—a principle that he is unequivocally committed to, but the religious man alone can justify adherence to this principle. The secularist is surreptitiously drawing on Christian inspiration when he insists that all men should be considered equal and that people's rights must be respected. For a secular morality to say all it wants and needs to say, it must, at this crucial point, be parasitical upon a God-centred morality. Without such a dependence on religion, secular morality collapses into egoism.

It may well be the case that, as a historical fact, our moral concern for persons came from our religious conceptions, but it is a well-known principle of logic that the validity of a belief is independent of its origin. What the religious moralist must do is to show that only on religious grounds could such a principle of respect for persons be justifiably asserted. But he has not shown that this is so; and there are good reasons for thinking that it is not so. Even if the secularist must simply subscribe to the Kantian principle, 'Treat every man as an end and never as a means only', as he must subscribe to the claim, 'Happiness is good', it does not follow that he is on worse ground than the religious moralist, for the religious moralist, too, as we have seen, must simply subscribe to his ultimate moral principle, 'Always do what God wills.'

In a way, the religious moralist's position here is simpler than the secularist's, for he needs only the fundamental moral principle that he ought to do what God wills. The secularist appears to need at least two fundamental principles. But in another and more important way the religious moralist's position is more complex, for he must subscribe to the extraordinarily obscure notion that man is a creature of God and as such has infinite worth. The Kantian principle may in the last analysis simply require subscription, but it is not inherently mysterious. To accept it does not require a crucifixion of the intellect. And if we are prepared simply to commit ourselves to one principle, why not to two principles, neither of which involves any appeal to conceptions whose very intelligibility is seriously in question?

The above argument is enough to destroy the believer's case here. But need we even rely on a historically religious concern as the basis for our moral position? There is a purely secular rationale for treating people fairly, for regarding them as persons. Let me show how this is so. We have no evidence that men ever lived in a pre-social state of nature. Man, as we know him, is an animal with a culture, he is part of a community, and the very concept of community implies binding principles and regulations—duties, obligations and rights. Yet, imaginatively we could conceive, in broad outline at any rate, what it would be like to live in a pre-social state.

In such a state no one would have any laws or principles to direct his behaviour. In that sense, man would be completely free. But such a life, as Hobbes graphically depicted, would be a clash of rival egoisms. Life in that state of nature would be, in his celebrated phrase, 'nasty, brutish and short'. Now if men were in such a state and if they were perfectly rational egoists, what kind of community life would they choose, given the fact that they were, very roughly speaking, nearly equal in strength and ability? (The fact that in communities as we find them men are not so nearly equal in power is beside the point for our hypothetical situation.) Given that they all start from scratch and have roughly equal abilities, it seems to me that it would be most reasonable, even for rational egoists, to band together into a community where each man's interests were given equal consideration, where each person was treated as deserving of respect.[5]

Each rational egoist would want others to treat him with respect, for his very happiness is contingent upon that; and he would recognize that he could attain the fullest cooperation of others only if other rational egoists knew or had good grounds for believing that their interests and their persons would also be respected. Such cooperation is essential for each egoist if all are to have the type of community life which would give them the best chance of satisfying their own interests to the fullest degree. Thus, even if men were thorough egoists, we would still have rational grounds for subscribing to a principle of respect for persons. That men are not thoroughly rational, do not live in a state of nature and are not thorough egoists does not gainsay the fact that we have rational grounds for regarding social life, organized in accordance with such a principle, as being objectively better than a social life which ignores this principle. The point here is that even rational egoists could see that this is the best possible social organization where men are nearly equal in ability.

What about the world we live in—a world in which, given certain extant social relationships, men are not equal or even nearly equal in power and opportunity? What reason is there for an egoist who is powerfully placed to respect the rights of others, when they cannot hurt him? We can say that his position, no matter how strong, might change and he might then need his rights protected; but this is surely not a strong enough reason for respecting human rights. To be moral involves respecting those rights, but our rational egoist may not propose to be moral. In considering such questions, we reach a point in reasoning at which we must simply decide what sort of person we shall strive to become. The religious moralist also reaches the same point. He, too, must make a decision of principle, but the principle he adopts is a fundamentally incoherent one. He not only must decide, but his decision must involve the acceptance of an absurdity.

It is sometimes argued by religious apologists that men will respect the rights of others only if they fear a wrathful and angry God. Without such a punitive sanction or threat, men will go wild. Yet it hardly seems to be the case that Christians, with their fear of hell, have been any better at respecting the rights of others than non-Christians. A study of the Middle Ages or the conquest of the non-Christian world makes this plain enough. And even if it were true that Christians were better in this respect than non-Christians, it would not show that they had a superior moral reason for their behaviour, for in so acting and in so reasoning, they are not giving a morally relevant reason at all but are simply acting out of fear for their own hides. Yet Christian morality supposedly takes us beyond the clash of the rival egoisms of secular life.

In short, Christian ethics has not been able to give us a sounder ground for respecting persons than we have with a purely secular morality. The Kantian principle of respect for persons is actually bound up in the very idea of morality, either secular or religious; and there are good reasons, of a perfectly mundane sort, why we should have the institution of morality as we now have it, namely, that our individual welfare is dependent on having a device which equitably resolves social and individual conflicts. Morality has an objective rationale in complete independence of religion. Even if God is dead, it does not really matter.

It is in just this last thrust, it might be objected, that you reveal your true colours and show your own inability to face a patent social reality. At this point the heart of your rationalism is very irrational. For millions of people, 'the death of God' means very much. It really does matter. In your somewhat technical sense, the concept of God may be chaotic or unintelligible, but this concept, embedded in our languages—embedded in 'the stream of life'—has an enormous social significance for many people. Jews and Christians, if they take their religion to heart, could not but feel a great rift in their lives with the loss of God, for they have indeed organized their lives around their religion. Their very life-ideals have grown out of these concepts. What should have been said is that if 'God is dead' it matters a lot, but nevertheless we should stand up like men and face this loss and learn to live in the Post-Christian era. As Nietzsche so well knew, to do this involves a basic reorientation of one's life and not just an intellectual dissent from a few statements of doctrine.

There is truth in such an objection and a kind of 'empiricism about man' that philosophers are prone to neglect. Of course it matters when one recognizes that one's religion is illusory. For a devout Jew or Christian to give up his God most certainly is important and does take him into the abyss of a spiritual crisis. But in saying that God's death does not really matter, I was implying what I have argued for in this essay; namely, that if an erstwhile believer loses his God but can keep his nerve, think the matter over and thoroughly take it to heart, life can still be meaningful and morality can yet have an objective rationale. Surely, for good psychological reasons, he is prone to doubt this argument, but if he will only 'hold on to his brains' and keep his courage, he will come to see that it is so. In this crucial sense it remains true that if 'God is dead' it does not really matter.

NOTES

[1] This is convincingly argued in Michael Scriven's 'Definitions, Explanations and Theories' in Feigl, H., Scriven, M. and Maxwell, G. (1958), *Minnesota Studies in the Philosophy of Science*, Minneapolis: University of Minnesota Press, vol. 2, pp 99–195

[2] I have argued this point in considerably more detail in Nielsen, Kai (1964), 'Linguistic Philosophy and "The Meaning of Life"' in *Cross Currents*, vol. XIV, no. 3, pp 313–34

[3] Moore, G. E. (1903), *Principia Ethica*, Cambridge: Cambridge University Press, chapters 1 and 2

[4] This crucial claim is ably argued by Nowell-Smith, P. H. (1957), *Ethics*, London: Blackwell, chapters 1–4; by Ladd, John (1953), 'Reason and Practice' in Wild, John (ed), *The Return to Reason*, Chicago: Chicago University Press, pp 253–358; and by Murphy, A. E., 'The Common Good' in *Proceedings and Addresses of the American Philosophy Association*, 1950–1, vol. XXIV, pp 3–18

[5] Some of the very complicated considerations relevant here have been brought out subtly by Rawls, John (1958), 'Justice as Fairness' in *The Philosophical Review*, vol. LXVII, pp 164–94, and by von Wright, Georg (1963), *The Varieties of Goodness*, London: Routledge, chapter 10. I think it could be reasonably maintained that my argument is more vulnerable here than at any other point. I would not, of course, use it if I did not think it could be sustained; but if anyone should find unconvincing the argument as presented here, I would beg him to consider the argument that precedes it and the one that immediately follows it. They alone are sufficient to establish my general case

FOUR

THE SEARCH FOR ABSOLUTES

I

IN THE LAST CHAPTER it was reasonably evident that my ethical theory relies on certain judgments about what is intrinsically good (about what is worth having or worth seeking for its own sake) in deciding what set of ultimate commitments are worthy of adoption or what set of aims a man should pursue. Happiness, self-consciousness, a sense of self-identity were the main candidates for intrinsic goodness. These things are taken to be intrinsically good because, when we are tolerably clear about the distinction between desiring something only as a means and desiring something as an end as well, they are what we would on reflection desire for their own sakes. Happiness, self-consciousness, a sense of self-identity are essential to give significance to human living; without them or the hope of their attainment, human life would not be worth living and bare human survival would be utterly pointless.

However, it is often thought that such a conception of the moral life has detestable implications which, when squarely faced, make it untenable. These implications apply to all such humanistic views which in crucial respects are heir to the assumptions of utilitarianism. And while my view is not, strictly speaking, utilitarian, it is close enough to it to share these defects or alleged defects.

What are these alleged defects which are supposed to undermine my view and even so humane a system of morality as I. S. Mill's? I am, in effect, giving you to understand that actions, rules, policies, practices and moral principles are ultimately to be judged by certain consequences: to wit, whether doing them more than, or at least as much as, doing anything else or acting in accordance with them more than, or at least as much as, acting in accordance with alternative principles, tends, on the whole, and for everyone involved, to maximize satisfaction, that is, to maximize happiness, minimize pain, enhance self-consciousness and preserve one's sense of self-identity. The states of affairs to be sought are those which maximize these things to the greatest extent possible for all mankind. But while this all sounds very humane and humanitarian, it has been forcefully argued that, when its implications are thought through, it will be seen actually to have inhumane and morally intolerable implications. On such a utilitarian or quasi-utilitarian view, circumstances *could* arise in which one would have to assert that one was justified in punishing, killing, torturing or deliberately harming the innocent and such a consequence is, morally speaking, unacceptable.[1] As Anscombe (whose views I discussed in Chapter One) has put it, anyone who 'really thinks, in advance, that it is open to question whether such an action as procuring the judicial execution of the innocent should be quite excluded from consideration—I do not want to argue with him; he shows a corrupt mind.'[2] Presumably such a view as I have been arguing has horrendous consequences; when I and others committed to such utilitarian or quasi-utilitarian ethical theories become fully aware of such consequences, we will abandon, if we have any moral sensitivity, nay, any plain humanity at all, such wayward ethical theories.

At the risk of being thought to exhibit a corrupt mind and a shallow consequentialist morality, I should like to argue that things are not as simple and straightforward as Anscombe seems to believe.

Surely every moral man must be appalled at the judicial execution of the innocent or at the punishment, torture and killing of the innocent. Indeed, being appalled by such behaviour partially defines what it is to be a moral agent. And I, as well as the utilitarian, have very good utilitarian grounds for being so appalled, namely, that it is always wrong to inflict pain for its own sake. But this does not get to the core considerations which divide a Christian absolutism such as Anscombe's from a humanist and quasi-utilitarian account of morality such as my own. There is a series of tough cases that need to be taken to heart and their implications thought through by any reflective person interested in morality, with or without God. By such investigation we can get to the heart of the issue between such an absolutism and my kind of consequentialism. Consider this clash between moral absolutism and utilitarianism arising over the problem of a 'just war'.

> If we deliberately bomb civilian targets, we do not pretend that civilians are combatants in any simple fashion, but argue that this bombing will terminate hostilities more quickly, and will minimize all around suffering. It is hard to see how any brand of utilitarianism will escape Miss Anscombe's objections. We are certainly killing the innocent . . . we are not killing them for the sake of killing them, but to save the lives of other innocent persons. Utilitarians, I think, grit their teeth and put up with this as part of the logic of total war; Miss Anscombe and anyone who thinks like her surely has to either redescribe the situation to ascribe guilt to the civilians or else she has to refuse to accept this sort of military tactic as simply wrong.[3]

It is indeed true that we cannot but feel the force of Miss Anscombe's objections. But is it the case that anyone shows a corrupt mind if he defends such bombing when, horrible as it is, it will quite definitely lessen appreciably the total amount of suffering and death in the long run, and if he is sufficiently non-evasive not to rationalize such a bombing of civilians into a situation in which all the putatively innocent people—children and all—are somehow in some measure judged guilty? Must it be the case that he exhibits a corrupt moral sense if he refuses to hold that such military tactics are never morally justified? Must this be the monstrous view of a fanatical man devoid of any proper moral awareness? It is difficult for me to believe that this must be so.

Consider the quite parallel actions of guerrilla fighters and

terrorists in wars of national liberation. In certain, almost
unavoidable circumstances, they must deliberately kill the
innocent. We need to see some cases in detail here to get the
necessary contextual background and for this reason the motion
picture, *The Battle of Algiers*, can be taken as a convenient point
of reference. In that film Algerian women—gentle women
with children of their own and plainly people of moral
sensitivity—with evident heaviness of heart, planted bombs
which they had every reason to believe would kill innocent
people, including children; a French general, also a human
being of moral fibre and integrity, ordered the torture of Arab
terrorists or suspected terrorists and threatened the bombing of
houses in which terrorists were concealed but which also
contained innocent people, including children. There are indeed many people involved in such activities who are cruel,
sadistic beasts or simply largely morally indifferent or, in
important ways, morally uncomprehending. But the characters
I referred to from *The Battle of Algiers* were not of that stamp.
They were moral agents of a high degree of sensitivity and yet
they deliberately killed or were prepared to kill the innocent.
And, with insignificant variations, this is a recurrent pheno-
menon of human living in extreme situations. Such cases are
by no means desert island or esoteric cases.

It is indeed arguable that such actions are always morally
wrong—whether anyone should ever act as the Arab women
or French general acted. But what could not be reasonably
maintained, *pace* Anscombe, by any stretch of the imagination
is that the characters I described from *The Battle of Algiers*
exhibited corrupt minds. Possibly morally mistaken yes,
guilty of moral corruption no.

Dropping the charge of moral corruption, but sticking with
the moral issue about what actions are right, is it not the case
that my consequentialist position logically forces me to conclude that under some circumstances—where the good to be
achieved is great enough—I must not only countenance but

actually advocate such violence toward the innocent? But is it not always, no matter what the circumstances or consequences, wrong even to countenance such violence, let alone to speak of advocating it or engaging in it? To answer such a question affirmatively is to commit oneself to the kind of moral absolutism which Miss Anscombe advocates. Given the alternatives, should not one be such an absolutist or at least hold that certain deontological principles (principles of right and wrong) must never be overridden?

I will take the papal bull by the horns, so to speak, and answer that there are circumstances when such violence must be reluctantly assented to or even taken to be something that one, morally speaking, must do. This very much needs arguing and I shall argue it, but first I would like to set out some further cases which have a similar bearing. They are by contrast artificial cases. Some of them, for someone who has a macabre sense of humour, might even seem funny, but I use them not to cause offence or to engage in a form of sick humour; rather, with their greater simplicity, by contrast with my above examples, there are fewer variables to control and I can more readily make the essential conceptual and moral points. But I shall neither forget nor neglect our more complex case.

II
Consider the following rather varied cases embedded in their exemplary tales.

1 *The Case of the Innocent Fat Man*
Consider the story (well known to philosophers) of the fat man stuck in the mouth of a cave on a coast. He was leading a group of people out of the cave when he stuck in the mouth of the cave. In a very short time high tide will be upon them and unless he is promptly unstuck, they all will be drowned except the fat man, whose head is out of the cave. Fortunately or unfortunately, someone has with him a stick of dynamite. The

short of the matter is, either they use the dynamite and blast the poor innocent fat man out of the mouth of the cave or everyone else drowns; either one life or many lives.

Our Christian absolutist presumably would take the attitude that it is all in God's hands and say that they ought never to blast the fat man out, for it is always wrong to kill the innocent. Must or should a moral man come to that conclusion? I shall argue that he should not.

2 The Case of the Dispensable Oldster

There are five shipwrecked people on a liferaft. All are of sound health, with people who love and depend on them at home, except for one ill old man slowly dying of cancer and whose relatives and close friends are all dead. Suppose further that the sea is getting rough and that it is as evident as anything can be that (a) they will not soon be rescued and (b) unless one man gets out into the freezing waters, the raft will be swamped.

Suppose they deliberate about what to do. If they do and they do it honestly and if the situation is as I have hypothesized, it seems to me perfectly evident that if they are deliberating morally, they should all decide—innocent though he is—that the old man should be sacrificed (he should jump overboard); and that if he does not agree to this that he should be forced to go overboard.[4] In the first instance, an innocent man is allowed to die (we forbear to prevent his death) and in the second instance (where he is forced overboard) an innocent man is killed. In the last instance we have gone against the principle of some Christian absolutists that the direct intention of the death of an innocent person is never justifiable. The rationale for what from a Christian point of view is a thoroughly immoral action is that moral reflection on the balance of good over evil makes it evident that this course of action is required from the moral point of view. The suffering and death of the innocent man is evil enough, but the more extensive death and suffering resulting from his not killing himself or being killed is a still worse evil. Ask yourself, if you were that old man what you would feel incumbent on yourself to do.

3 *Der Übermensch on a Liferaft*

There are two men in a liferaft. One is simply a plain man (a plain banker, teacher, car dealer, trolley-car conductor), the other a scientist on the verge of making a major discovery in cancer research which will lead to a breakthrough in the treatment of cancer. Where it is impossible that they both can live in such a situation, a consequentialist ethic like my own is committed to saying that the scientist should protect his life even by killing the plain man, if it becomes necessary.

Many regard this attitude as morally offensive. All people, it is maintained, are of equal worth and have equal rights. We cannot simply sacrifice another man in such a manner. Morally speaking, we cannot simply sacrifice him in any manner. That people in life and in *The Last Exit to Brooklyn* are treated differently only proves what any tolerably realistic man should know: the moral ordering of things is frequently grossly disregarded. To think that we can justifiably sacrifice a man in this way is to abandon moral principle and, we are told, to play God. It is never right to sacrifice an innocent man to rescue another no matter who that other man is and no matter how essential he is to the community. And the evil is even greater when a man sacrifices another innocent man to save himself. Again, I think such religiose moral absolutism is mistaken and I shall attempt to show why when I have all our exemplary tales before us.

4 *The Mad Matriarch*

Consider a not exactly typical group of people living on a small island. (A kind of miniature Haiti, let us say.) Suppose the island is poverty-stricken and very backward and has been dominated for centuries by one dictatorial family. Things in recent years have gone from bad to worse and the island, ruled single-handedly by a mad old matriarch—the last member of the ruling dynasty—is now reduced to starvation and disease. And she is so mad that she cannot be made to understand what is happening to the population on the island and will not release money in her possession which could be used to buy supplies which will halt the starvation and enable the island to begin to recover. She is untouchable by the masses of the people for she is thought, as has been believed about the ruling dynasty for as long as anyone can remember, to be a holy witch who can hex anything and destroy at will. It is even almost universally believed by the islanders that to kill her will bring devastation to the island through unleashing the wrath of the evil spirits. Thus her bodyguards remain loyal to her and the population, no matter how bad things get, will not revolt against her. Do not forget that the old woman is not a vicious old woman, just utterly mad. She thinks that by holding on to the money come what may, she is saving the precious heritage of her land. She cannot be prevailed on to part with the money and the population cannot be brought to touch the money while the holy witch lives.

Unless we are to play with words, we should admit that she is an innocent person. After all, she is not responsible for her actions. But suppose you were an intellectual and concerned human being in that country, free from its tribal mythology. What should you try to do? If you hold the kind of normative ethical view I hold and there were no way of saving the starving people other than by killing (murdering, if you will) the old woman, would it not be something you plainly ought to do? I think it is, yet this runs foul of the moral principle of Anscombean Christian absolutism that the direct intention of the death of an innocent person is never justifiable. Again, who is right here? Can anyone be shown to be right or have we come to such fundamental moral differences that we have arrived at differences in moral posture which are unarguable?

I think these differences are arguable and that my consequentialist attitude is the right one. In section IV of this chapter I shall turn to that argument.

My exemplary tales so far have been of the kind designed to show that our normal immediate rather absolutist moral reactions need to be questioned along with such principles as 'The direct intention of the death of an innocent person is never justifiable.' I have hinted (and later shall argue) that we should beware of our moral outrage here—our naturally conservative and unreflective moral reactions—for here the consequentialist has a strong case for what I shall call moral radicalism. But before turning to a defence of that, I want to tell three more stories, all taken from Phillipa Foot, but used for my own purposes.[5] These tales, I shall argue, have a different import from our previous tales, for with them I think our unrehearsed, common-sense moral reactions will stand up under moral scrutiny. I shall also argue, when I consider them in section III, that our common-sense moral reactions here, initial expectations to the contrary notwithstanding, can be shown to be justified on consequentialist grounds. The thrust of my argument concerning both sets of cases is that in neither are we justified in opting for a theistic and/or deontological absolutism or in rejecting consequentialism. But to return to our remaining exemplary tales.

5 The Magistrate and the Threatening Mob

A magistrate or judge is faced with a very real threat from a large and uncontrollable mob of rioters demanding a culprit for a crime. Unless the criminal is produced, promptly tried and executed, they will take their own bloody revenge on a much smaller and quite vulnerable section of the community (a kind of frenzied pogrom). The judge knows that the real culprit is unknown and that the authorities do not even have a good clue as to whom he may be. But he also knows that

D

there is within easy reach a disreputable, thoroughly disliked and useless man who, though innocent, could easily be framed so that the mob would be quite convinced that he was guilty and would be pacified if he were promptly executed. Recognizing that he can prevent the occurrence of extensive carnage only by framing some innocent person, the magistrate has him framed, goes through the mockery of a trial and has him executed.

Most of us regard the framing and execution of such a man in such circumstances as totally unacceptable. There are some who would say that it is categorically wrong—morally inexcusable—whatever the circumstances. Indeed, such a case remains a problem for the consequentialist, but here again, I shall argue, one can consistently remain a consequentialist and continue to accept common-sense moral convictions about such matters.

6 *The Indispensable Serum*

Suppose that several dangerously ill people can be saved only if we kill a certain individual and use his diseased dead body in the preparation of a serum. But we immediately, and, on reflection as well, feel, as Foot observes, that we would not in anything even approximating a realistic situation be justified in killing a man for such purposes. I think that our convictions here are correct, and I shall argue that we can give good consequentialist reasons for sticking by the moral dictates of common-sense morality.[6]

7 *The Teleological Torturer*

Suppose we have the good fortune to live in a quite open tyranny such as, for example, Greece, Spain, Portugal or South Africa, and that we are faced with a moral dilemma forced on us by the fiendish local representative of the leader. This beastly man presents one of us, as a representative member of the dwindling intelligentsia, with the following (as far as can be discerned) thoroughly earnest proposal: unless we torture one innocent man, our *kleiner Fuehrer* will, with even greater torment than he requires of us, torture five men to death. That is, one member of the intelligentsia is singled out for harassment; unless he tortures one man, five others will be tortured and killed.

If one were the person selected for this harassment, would it not be one's duty, on such an ethical theory as the one I argued for in Chapter Three, to torture one man to keep the other five from being tortured to death? I shall argue that it is neither one's duty nor even something which one is morally justified in doing.

My cycle of little moral tales is at an end. The task is to see what they imply. We must try to determine whether thinking through their implications should lead a clear-headed and morally sensitive man to abandon the kind of humanistic and teleological framework I have given to normative ethics and to adopt some form of theistic absolutism and/or deontological absolutism. I shall argue that it does not.

III

I shall consider the last three cases first because there are good reasons why the consequentialist should stick with common-sense moral convictions in such cases. I shall start by giving my rationale for that claim. Consider case 5, the case of the magistrate and the threatening mob. If the magistrate were a tough-minded but morally conscientious utilitarian, he could on straightforward utilitarian grounds refuse to frame and execute the innocent man even knowing that this would unleash the mob (note that in practice it would be very unlikely that he could know that) and cause much suffering and many deaths.

The rationale for his particular moral stand would be that by so framing and then executing such an innocent man, he

would in the long run cause still more suffering, through the
resultant corrupting effect on the institution of justice. That is
to say, in a case involving such extensive general interest in the
issue—without that there would be no problem in preventing
the carnage and no call for such extreme measures—knowledge
that the man was framed, that the law had prostituted itself,
would surely eventually leak out. This would encourage mob
action in other circumstances; it would lead to an increased
scepticism about the incorruptibility or even the reliability of
the judicial process, and it would set a dangerous precedent for
less clear-headed or less scrupulously humane magistrates.
Given such a potential for the corruption of justice, a utilitarian or consequentialist judge or magistrate could on good
utilitarian or consequentialist grounds argue that it was
morally wrong to frame an innocent man. If the mob will
rampage if such a sacrificial lamb is not provided, then the
mob must rampage.

Must a utilitarian or consequentialist come to such a conclusion? The answer is no. It is the conclusion which is, as
things stand, the most reasonable conclusion to come to, but
that he must come to it is far too strong a claim. A utilitarian
could consistently—I did not say successfully—argue that our
tough-minded utilitarian magistrate had overestimated the
corrupting effects of such judicial railroading. His circumstance
was an extreme one, a situation not often to be repeated even
if, instead of acting as he did, he had set a precedent by such an
act of judicial murder. If that is in fact so, a utilitarian could
reason that since very many innocent people would otherwise
be murdered and given a firm understanding that this really
is the case, the institution of justice would not be extensively
harmed at all by such a surreptitious judicial murder. Indeed, a
grave injustice with vile consequences would be wrought on
one individual, but even worse consequences would follow
if the mob were allowed to rampage. Such a utilitarian
magistrate would insist that the judicial murder of one

innocent man is the lesser evil; and that the lesser evil is always to be preferred to the greater.

The short of it is, that utilitarians could disagree, as other consequentialists could disagree, about what is morally required of us in that case. The disagreement here between utilitarians or consequentialists of the same type is not one concerning fundamental moral principles but a disagreement about the empirical facts, about what course of action will in the long run produce the least suffering and the most happiness for everyone involved. (Given the kind of consequentialism I defended in Chapter Three, intrinsic goods other than happiness would have to be brought in as well and *everyone's* interests would have to be considered.[7] This would complicate the above statement but would not change the essentials of the dispute. For convenience of expression, but for no other reason, I will continue to put the matter in this utilitarian manner.)

However, considering the effect that advocating the deliberate judicial killing of an innocent man would have on people's reliance on common-sense moral beliefs of such a ubiquitous sort as the belief that the innocent must not be harmed, a utilitarian who defended the centrality of common-sense moral beliefs would indeed have a strong utilitarian case here. But the most crucial thing to recognize is that to regard such judicial bowing to such a threatening mob as unqualifiedly wrong, as morally intolerable, one need not reject utilitarianism and accept some form of theistic or deontological absolutism.

It may be argued that in taking such a stance I still have not squarely faced the absolutist's objection to the judicial railroading of the innocent. I allow, as a consequentialist, that there could be circumstances, at least as far as logical possibilities are concerned, in which such a railroading would be justified but that as things actually go, it is not and probably never in fact will be justified. But the absolutist's point is that in no circumstances, either actual or conceivable, would it be justified. No matter what the consequences, it is unqualifiedly unjustified. To say, as I do, that the situations in which it might be justified are desert-island, esoteric cases which do not occur in life, is not to the point, for, as Alan Donagan argues, 'moral theory is *a priori*, as clear-headed utilitarians like Henry Sidgwick recognized. It is, as Leibniz would say, "true of all possible worlds".'[8] Thus to argue as I have that the counter-examples directed against consequentialists appeal to conditions which are never in fact fulfilled or are unlikely to be fulfilled is beside the point.[9] Whether 'a moral theory is true or false depends on whether its implications for all possible worlds are true. Hence, whether utilitarianism (or consequentialism) is true or false cannot depend on how the actual world is.'[10] It is possible to specify logically conceivable situations in which consequentialism would have implications which are monstrous, for example, certain beneficial judicial murders of the innocent (whether they are even remotely likely to obtain is irrelevant), hence consequentialism must be false.

We should not take such a short way with consequentialists, for what is true in Donagan's claim about moral theory being *a priori* will not refute or even render implausible consequentialism; and what would undermine it in such a claim about the *a priori* nature of moral theory and presumably moral claims is not true. To say that moral theory is *a priori* is probably correct if that means that categorical moral claims —fundamental moral statements—cannot be deduced from empirical statements or non-moral theological statements such that it is a contradiction to assert the empirical and/or non-moral theological statements and deny the categorical moral claims or vice versa.[11] In that fundamental sense it is reasonable, and, I believe, justified, to maintain that moral theory is autonomous and *a priori*. It is also *a priori* in the sense that moral statements are not themselves a kind of empirical statement. That is, if I assert 'One ought to respect an individual's rights' or 'One ought to protect an innocent man', I am not trying to predict or describe what people do or are likely to do, but am asserting what they are to do. It is also true that if a moral statement is true, it holds for all possible worlds in which situations of exactly the sort characterized in the statement obtain. If it is true for one, it is true for all. You cannot consistently say that A ought to do B in situation Y and deny that someone exactly like A in a situation exactly like Y ought to do B.

In these ways moral claims and indeed moral theory are *a priori*. But it is also evident that none of these ways will touch the consequentialist or utilitarian arguments. After all, the utilitarian need not be and typically has not been an ethical naturalist—he need not think moral claims are derivable from factual claims or that moral claims are a subspecies of empirical statement; and he could accept (indeed, he must accept) what is an important truism anyway—that you cannot consistently say that A ought to do B in situation Y and deny that someone exactly like A in a situation exactly like Y ought to do B. But he could and should deny that moral claims are *a priori* in the sense that rational men must or even will make them without regard for the context in which they are made. We say people ought not to exceed the speed limit or speed on icy roads or throw knives at each other. But if human beings had a kind of metallic exoskeleton and would not be hurt, disfigured or seriously inconvenienced by knives sticking in them or by automobile crashes, we would not so evidently at least have good grounds for saying that such speeding or knife-throwing is wrong. It would not be so obviously unreasonable and immoral to do these things if those conditions obtained.

In the very way we choose to describe the situation when we make ethical remarks, it is important in making this choice that we know what the world is like and what human beings are like. Our understanding of the situation, our understanding of human nature and motivation, cannot but effect our structuring of the moral case. Consider the difference between how psychologically secure, knowledgeable persons and uneducated, psychologically insecure persons characterize sexual offences. What sickens and saddens one man and makes him hope all the more for better conditions of detection and cure of the criminally insane drives another to rage and to demand prompt justice through the use of the death penalty. To recognize and stress the relevance of our knowledge of human nature in the making of moral assessments is perfectly compatible with a recognition, as we find it, for example, in Hume, that moral claims are not empirical claims and that no fundamental moral claim is entailed by an empirical claim.

The consequentialist is saying that, as the world goes, there are good grounds for holding that judicial killings are morally intolerable, though he would have to admit that if the world were very different, they could be something that ought to be done. But in holding this, he is not committed to denying the universalizability of moral judgments, for where he would reverse or qualify the moral judgment, the situation must be different. He is only committed to claiming that where the situation is the same or relevantly similar and the persons are relevantly similar, they must, if they are to act morally, do the same thing. He is claiming that, as things stand, judicial killing of the innocent is always wrong and he is affirming that it is an irrational moral judgment to assert of a reasonably determinate action (for example, killing an innocent man) that it is unjustifiable and morally unacceptable in all possible worlds, whatever the situation and whatever the consequences.

Perhaps such a consequentialist claim with its recognition that we must not make moral judgments without careful attention to context, is in some way mistaken. I am not at all convinced that this is so. On the contrary, it seems to me an important truth about the nature of morality. But whether I am right about this or not, Donagan's claims about the *a priori* nature of moral theories do not show such a claim to be mistaken or even give us the slightest reason for thinking that it is mistaken. What is brutal and vile, for example, throwing a knife at a human being just for the fun of it, would not be so, if human beings were invulnerable to harm from such a direction because they had a metallic exoskeleton. Similarly, what is, as things are, morally intolerable, for example, the judicial killing of the innocent, need not be morally intolerable in all conceivable worlds.

Similar things should be said about case 6, the case of the indispensable serum. Suppose a new kind of deadly plague is raging in Basel, killing people left and right and that we need to kill a living human who is in a certain stage of the disease to make a serum to halt the plague. Suppose, further, that given the present development of science, this is the only way such a serum could be made. An old man, quite alone in the world and miserable, has contracted the plague and is very likely to die from it and is in the right stage. How can we, given that we are consequentialists and that the plague so virulently stalks the land, deny that we should kill him? A utilitarian, who also remained committed to our common-sense moral convictions about killing innocent people, could reply that the very central importance in morality—including utilitarian morality—of respect for life makes such killing morally unthinkable. As in the case of the magistrate and the threatening mob, respect for justice was at issue, so in the case of the indispensable serum, respect for persons, for life itself, is at issue. We human beings would not want—indeed, could not morally tolerate—a world in which human life and human rights were treated so lightly. We cannot, from a moral point of view, regard a man as a means only. A world in which this was so is not a world in which a moral order prevails and it is not a world in which people could be happy or attain self-fulfilment, so there are very good consequentialist grounds for not preparing a serum—no matter how indispensable—if it is necessary to kill an innocent man to do this.

Again, I do not mean that a consequentialist must accept this particular judgment about serum making but that a consequentialist consistently and plausibly can accept it. Indeed, a consequentialist such as myself who qualified utilitarianism by stressing that it is not enough just to seek maximization of human happiness or satisfaction of desire and minimization of suffering, but that we must maximize and minimize it fairly so that everyone's interests are equally taken into consideration, puts critical weight on the notion of respect for persons. This is what such a qualification of utilitarianism stresses. No one, from a moral point of view, can be left out of account. This is what in essence should be meant by the claim that no one can be treated as a means only.

However, that everyone's interests must be considered does not mean that where there are irreconcilable conflicts of interest, no particular interests should take pride of place. Morality in part exists to give us some means of making a just and humane resolution where there are such conflicts of interest. What it does require is that in moral deliberation, every man's interests must be considered and given an initial equal weight. Departures from the initial positions of equality in the form of special treatment for certain individuals (for example, everything else being equal, a mother with small children rather than an unmarried person should be given first choice for a scarce place in a lifeboat), must be capable of being given general justification (for example, that, everything else being equal, the same thing holds for anyone who is a mother with small children and for anyone who is unmarried). The resultant positions of inequality (both advantageous and disadvantageous) must be open to all. (By saying that they are open to all, I mean that someone cannot claim them simply on hereditary or racial grounds or, at least for the vast majority of cases, on grounds by which a person by his own good effort could not be in a position to achieve.) Thus, in reasoning morally we must start from a position in which man's interests are to be given equal weight; all subsequent qualifications of this must be fair; that is, they must be in accordance with general principles of justice and equality. Where there are irreconcilable conflicting interests, some sacrifice of interest must be made. The point is to make such necessary sacrifices in as fair and humane a way as possible.

However, even when operating, as I do, from this kind of consequentialist position, one is not *logically* forced, from the weight one gives to the principle of respect for persons, to say that such serum making must be morally intolerable in all conceivable circumstances. Surely the sceptic can ask, how we can be so sure that we—that is, humanity generally—would be happier or would attain greater self-fulfilment in a world made safe from such serum makers? Recall that we say that no man can be treated as a means *only*. When in our situation a man is made serum of, he is not treated as a means *only*. His person is still respected; he is not picked out simply because he is John Jones, a black, poor, conveniently at hand or the like. In fact, in such a situation, one would expect a very moral and very strong man to offer up his life. That he is killed rather than someone else, our sceptical utilitarian will argue, is something that has a rationale which, though it sanctions the taking of innocent life, could still be plausibly argued to be just; and there are humane reasons why his life is taken rather than someone else's. Is it so evident, when it is carefully thought through, that such a killing of an innocent person is never justifiable? Is it so evident that no logically possible situation could arise in which it would be justified? It is not evident to me that we should answer these questions in the negative.

We very rightly feel utter horror at such a taking of life. But think of the people we allow to die by not killing the man. The usual remark to make here is that we do not intend their death while we deliberately kill the man, and that, it is often said, makes all the difference in the world. There indeed is an important distinction between avoiding harming or killing someone, on the one hand, and bringing aid, on the other. The moral imperative to do the former is normally stronger than the moral imperative to do the latter. There is no doubt always something that someone could do to help save lives somewhere, but this claim of others is not as strong as the claim they have on our forbearing to harm them.

However, while this distinction is a significant one, it is not clear how far it will carry us in considering the present case. If a plague were killing people everywhere and there were no other way of saving vast numbers of people except by such a ghastly serum making, would it then be so evidently wrong to do it? I know well enough, if I had the plague in the right stage, were old and ill (perhaps even if I were not old and ill) and there were no other person or no community in a similar state, willing to draw straws, I would feel it morally incumbent on myself to sacrifice myself. If that is a reasonable moral sentiment and not just an expression of a sick martyr complex and if I am not ill with the plague, but someone else is who fits the description under which I would rightly be prepared to sacrifice myself except that he will not volunteer for the sacrifice, is it so plainly wrong to say that he should be killed?

If we have anything at all approximating moral sensitivity, we reel at the thought of killing someone and there are strong consequentialist reasons against such serum making. If we believe in God, I suppose, it is reasonable to assert 'It is all in the hands of God. By not killing, I have harmed no man,' and to refrain categorically from such serum making.[12] A secularist, however, cannot so easily escape responsibility. That he cannot and that it is difficult to live with that responsibility is perhaps part of what Nietzsche meant when he said that we must learn to transvaluate values in a world without God. Indeed, it is true that by advocating the killing of someone or by killing someone himself, he wrongly injures that person and perhaps by refraining from action and thus forbearing to prevent many deaths no one is injured by him. No one can justifiably make a claim on the serum-forbearer that he owed him the serum, but still by so acting we who are serum-forbearers are responsible for allowing the plague to rage out of control, among ourselves and our children: the latter being particularly important here for they have no choice in the matter.

Such considerations support the utilitarian or consequentialist sceptical of the claims of our common-sense morality. Yet it may also well be the case—given our extensive cruelty anyway—that, if we ever start sanctioning such behaviour, an even greater callousness toward life will develop than the very extensive callousness extant now. Given a normative ethical theory which sanctions such serum-making behaviour under certain circumstances, there may occur an undermining of our moral disapproval of killing and our absolutely essential moral principle that all human beings, great and small, are deserving of respect. This is surely enough, together with the not unimportant weight of even our unrehearsed moral feelings, to give strong utilitarian weight here to the dictates of our common-sense morality. Yet I think I have also said enough to show that someone who questions their 'unquestionableness' in such a context does not thereby exhibit a 'corrupt mind' and that it is an open question whether he must be conceptually confused over this matter if he does not have a 'corrupt mind'. Still, to put it most conservatively, the consequentialist who remains committed to what I have called a common-sense moral commitment has not been exposed as being inconsistent or somehow confused and vacillating.

The case of the teleological torturer, case 7, can be handled with greater brevity than the case of the indispensable serum for very similar considerations apply in both cases. However, the former merits independent consideration because it reveals a feature of many puzzle-cases which would lead a reasonable consequentialist in considering such cases to defend sticking with common-sense moral convictions. Case 7 was the case where a mad and fiendish tyrant demands that we torture one innocent man or he will torture even more fiercely five men. In this case, consequentialists should absolutely refuse to be teleological torturers and for eminently practical reasons: given a man who is sufficiently mad and morally depraved to make such a demand, we could have no confidence at all that he would stick by his promise and not torture them and others as well after we had done our own horrified torturing to try to lessen the balance of evil resulting from his horrible threat. In such a Caligula-situation, nothing is sufficiently stable to enable us to have even a tolerably steadfast confidence in the tyrant's promises or commitments. Given the enormity of what we are asked to do, given the plain evil and swinishness of it, it is not something the toughest utilitarian would be justified in doing in such a precarious situation. In addition, there are features here that we noted obtained also in the serum case and which strengthen a utilitarian defence of sticking, in such a situation, by our common-sense moral convictions.

It is time now that we look at a reply to what I have been arguing in discussing cases 5, 6 and 7. I shall call it the desert islander argument. Suppose, referring to the case of the teleological torturer, someone says, but what would be the right thing to do if one could be quite confident that our *kleiner Fuehrer* would keep his promise and torture the five others horribly? Suppose there was a precedent here resulting from the fact that the horrible practice had been developed and sustained through the brutal power of the tyranny for some considerable time. Would you not then have good grounds for believing him and then must you not in such a situation, if you care to remain a consistent consequentialist, reluctantly torture to prevent still more evil? Surely it is natural to reply that such monstrous activities, evil in themselves, also have evil side effects, for example, they brutalize one, make one increasingly insensitive to pain and bring out pervasive latent sadistic impulses which normally are more readily held in check. Such considerations surely strengthen the case for the utilitarian trying to defend common-sense moral convictions, but the determined desert islander can always persist by asking 'But what if it would not have such brutalizing side effects?' Must not a consistent consequentialist then become in such a circumstance a teleological torturer?

Suppose we *know* that unless we sawed off a man's arm a tyrant would torture to death a whole town. Should we not then become teleological torturers? Similarly, in response to our utilitarian defence of the case of the magistrate and the threatening mob, the desert islander can ask: 'But should not a consistent consequentialist judicially murder such innocent men, when and if he could be perfectly confident that knowledge of it or even rumour of it would not leak out, that it would not have a corrupting effect on him or others and generally that it would not have a corrupting effect on the institution of justice?' And again with the case of the indispensable serum, suppose the situation was very tight: (a) the new plague was spreading out from Basel to all of central Europe, (b) the killing in such a situation of an innocent man would not so harden one morally or have dangerous political side effects, and (c) that it was quite clear that this was the only way for the next hundred years to make such a serum. If this wildly fanciful situation were the real situation, should we not indeed kill him, if we stick by our consequentialist moral principles.

It is indeed true that by heaping on enough conditions the desert islander can always produce a conflict between utilitarianism (or other forms of consequentialism) and certain of our common-sense moral convictions or principles, such as the deep-seated conviction that the direct intention of the death of an innocent person is never justifiable. If we are consequentialists, there are logically possible situations in which we must admit that such behaviour would be required of us.

But such a possibility, it is argued, is sufficient to discredit such an ethical theory.

There are several things that need to be said about such desert islander arguments. It needs to be carefully noted how unrealistically full of 'ifs' the situations are where cases 5, 6 and 7 would produce at least an apparent conflict between our common-sense moral principles and a reflective consequentialism. Moral discourse is fitted for the recurrent practical situations of life and not for such wildly improbable situations as determined desert islanders foist upon us. We might no more know what to say here than we would know what to say in tennis if someone made a very high serve and the ball, without going out of the court, went up and up and we waited two hours and it still had not come down. How are we to count that serve? Is it a fault? The rules were not made to cover such contingencies, such a desert island situation, but there is nothing wrong with them for all that. Similarly in the moral case, in some wildly improbable desert island situations we very well might not know what to say. Moral discourses and moral concepts are none the worse for that.

Such remarks might still be felt to be failing to meet the objection. It is tempting to reply to my above rejection of desert island cases, that nevertheless we understand the conditions and if, *per impossible* if you will, they were to obtain, we can see that on consequentialist principles such swinish acts would be required of us and that they are so evil that they would never be justified or even morally tolerable. This is precisely—the argument would continue—the value of desert island cases. They bring out what otherwise might be obscured. Thus they are not irrelevant after all.

However, if the desert islander's game is played and we do consider what moral conclusions we should come to about such exotically improbable cases, then we should realize that sticking with the principles of common-sense theistic or deontological absolutism is not so obviously the best or right thing to do. Playing that game we need to take the following desert island cases seriously; and, when we treat them in that way, it is again not obvious that the consequentialist is mistaken. What should we do if it were the case that a whole nation would perish if one innocent man were not murdered, a million innocent people would be killed if a magistrate did not, through fool-proof manipulation, get an innocent man convicted of murder, or a thousand children would be tortured to death if we did not pull out the fingernails of one innocent man? These are all cases, *if* we take them seriously, where it is not at all obvious that we must, on pain of moral error or corruption of mind, stick to absolutistic or Christian deontological principles. If we set aside such desert island cases as irrelevant to moral reflection, as I suggest we should, the consequentialist's position is a strong one. But he is also in a strong position if we nevertheless choose to utilize these cases and really think through what they would involve.

There will indeed be borderline cases which are not quite so 'iffy' as the most paradigmatic desert island cases in which, if they were to become real-life situations, we would be in an agonizing moral perplexity. They would be situations in which we would not know what to say or what moral course to take.[13] But that some situations should lead us into such moral surds should not be surprising. Morality is a very complex form of life. There could hardly be a decision procedure here with the precision of the propositional calculus. Moral principles, except, perhaps, such consumately general ones as the principles of utility, justice and respect for persons, are such that they are tailored to recurrent situations which arise in human living. In such situations, we have good utilitarian and consequentialist grounds for acting in accordance with pervasive common-sense moral dictates of the type discussed.

However, right here, another difficulty becomes evident. It is not unnatural to say that such a contingent defence of such common-sense moral principles is not enough. In discussing the case of the magistrate and the threatening mob and the case of the indispensable serum, I admitted that, depending on their judgments about the empirical facts and the acuteness of their thinking through the implications of their moral postures and their knowledge of men and affairs, conscientious utilitarians and other consequentialists might disagree about what ought to be done in such cases. But if they may so disagree, if a conscientious consequentialist is not forced (logically compelled) to conclude that torturing an innocent person or procuring the judicial execution of the innocent must always be morally intolerable, then—so the objection runs—his position does not give us a sure moral foundation to condemn these things as being morally unthinkable. But, it may be argued, such an assurance is exactly what an adequate morality requires.

We have already seen how Miss Anscombe does not want to argue with such consequentialists, for she concludes from their very taking of such a posture toward the world that they have corrupt minds—that such people have monstrous moral views or are flagrantly disregarding moral considerations. Surely such Christian absolutists want a stronger, more certain foundation for such moral claims than the consequentialist one I gave. That the direct intention of the death of an innocent person is never morally justifiable must remain a closed question for them. To refuse to so treat it, according to them, must be either symptomatic of having an immoral moral code or of going beyond moral considerations altogether.

Since 'moral' contrasts with both 'immoral' and 'non-moral', there is nothing conceptually inappropriate about speaking of 'an immoral moral code' or of 'an immoral morality'. In so speaking, we are saying that a code which is admittedly a moral code, as opposed to a non-moral code, is unacceptable because, unlike a morally acceptable moral code, it is an evil, morally intolerable moral code. Thus someone who regards the sexual habits of the Tahitians as immoral might say consistently enough that Tahitians have an immoral sexual morality; and in Kafka's *Penal Colony*, the explorer gradually comes to understand that the officer has a severe, demanding and indeed universalizable moral code (he stoically applies it to himself when the occasion arises) containing a commitment to justice while remaining for all that a hideously and unbelievably inhumane morality.

It is not clear whether Christian and deontological absolutists such as Miss Anscombe regard such a consequentialist position as an immoral morality or as some kind of morally sick normative position beyond moral good and evil altogether. It would seem to me more reasonable to argue that it is an immoral morality than to deny that it is a morality at all. In either case, such an absolutism does not have much merit. To say that a consequentialist position is not any kind of moral position at all is surely implicitly to redefine, in a stipulative manner, the way we characterize the difference between a moral and a non-moral code. But even allowing this linguistic gerrymandering, nothing is accomplished, for with the narrowed conception of a moral code, the relevant question simply becomes whether, under all conditions, moral considerations should be definitive in determining how we ought to act. Perhaps, it will be queried, in some forms of the extreme situations represented by cases 5, 6 and 7, moral considerations should not be decisive. However, it is less muddling to regard such consequentialist codes as moral codes and to assert they are immoral moral codes rather than non-moral codes. That is to say, this is clearer and less arbitrary linguistically.

The important consideration surely is to get beyond Anscombean dogmatic moral assertion and show why such codes are immoral. It will be argued by all partners to this dispute that it is wrong directly to intend the death of an innocent person and that it is unjust to punish or harm someone for something he did not do or could not help doing. But consequentialists such as myself think that morally speaking it is an open question whether in certain very extreme circumstances, we should deliberately do what is wrong or unjust to prevent a still greater evil. Or to put it in a less paradoxical way, it is an open question whether in certain extreme circumstances, we should not do something which normally would be grossly wrong but is not so evidently wrong here because of the fact that by not doing it a still greater evil is obtained. Surely by giving up a rigid acceptance of the kind of deontological principles such absolutists follow, we have complicated moral decision. But a simpler system which stuck by absolutist principles no matter how much suffering or how much evil resulted would, to put it conservatively, be morally paradoxical. Surely the burden of argument is on such deontologists and Christian absolutists to show either (*a*) why one should not always act in accordance with the formula: where faced with two evils both of which cannot be avoided, do the lesser evil, or (*b*) why it never can be the case that acting unjustly or killing an innocent man is ever in any circumstance the lesser evil. Until such time as convincing argument is made here, the consequentialist argument appears at least to be very strong and it looks like the Christian absolutist is on a Quixotic and morally irresponsible quest for moral certainty and purity —a quest which will shield him from some very agonizing moral decisions but will hardly enable him to come to grips with some demanding moral dilemmas.

IV

So far, I have tried to show with reference to cases 5, 6 and 7 how consequentialists (including utilitarians) can reasonably square their normative ethical theories with an important range of common-sense moral convictions. Now, by reference to cases 1, 2, 3 and 4, I wish to establish that there is at least a serious question concerning whether such fundamental common-sense moral convictions should always function as moral facts or as a kind of moral ground to test the adequacy of philosophical moral (normative ethical) theories or positions. I want to establish that careful attention to such cases shows that we are not justified in taking the principles embodied in our common-sense moral reasoning about such cases as normative for all moral decisions. That a normative ethical theory is incompatible with some of our moral intuitions (moral feelings or convictions) does not refute the normative ethical theory. What I will try to do here is to establish whether these cases, any more than cases 5, 6 and 7 examined in section III, give us adequate grounds for abandoning the kind of teleological and humanistic normative ethic I argued for in Chapter Three and for adopting some theistic and/or deontological absolutism.

Forget the levity of the example and consider the case of the innocent fat man. If there really is no other way of unsticking our fat man and if plainly, without blasting him out, everyone in the cave will drown, then, innocent or not, he should be blasted out. This indeed overrides the principle that the innocent should never be deliberately killed; but it does not reveal a callousness toward life, for the people involved are caught in a desperate situation in which, if such extreme action is not taken, many lives will be lost and far greater misery will obtain. Moreover, the people who do such a horrible thing or acquiesce in the doing of it are not likely to be rendered more callous about human life and human suffering as a result. Its occurrence will haunt them for the rest of their lives and is as likely as not to make them more, rather than less, morally sensitive. (What is even more likely is that their subsequent behaviour will not be substantially effected at all.) It is not even correct to say that such a desperate act shows a lack of respect for persons. We are not treating the fat man merely as a means. The fat man's person—his interests and rights—are not ignored. Killing him is something which is undertaken with the greatest reluctance. It is only when it is quite certain that there is no other way to save the lives of the others that such a violent course of action is justifiably undertaken.

Alan Donagan,[14] arguing rather as Anscombe argues, maintains that 'to use any innocent man ill for the sake of some public good is directly to degrade him to being a mere means' and to do this is of course to violate a principle essential to morality and thus to my variety of consequentialism as well. But, as my above remarks show, it need not be the case, and in the above situation it is not the case, that in killing such an innocent man we are treating him merely as a means. The action is universalizable, all alternative actions which would save his life are duly considered, the blasting out is done only as a last and desperate resort with the minimum of harshness and indifference to his suffering and the like. It indeed sounds ironical to talk this way, given what is done to him. But if such a terrible situation were to arise, there would always be more or less humane ways of going about one's grim task. And in acting in the more humane ways toward the fat man, as we do what we must do and would have done to ourselves were the roles reversed, we show a respect for his person.[15]

In so treating the fat man—not just to further the public good but to prevent the certain death of a whole group of people (that is, to prevent an even greater evil than his being killed in this way)—the claims of justice are not overriden either, for each individual involved, if he is reasoning correctly, should realize that if he, rather than the fat man, were so stuck, he should in such a situation be blasted out. Thus there is no question of being unfair. And is there really a question of being brutish and inhumane when we consider that by not so acting many people are in effect condemned to death? Surely we must choose between evils here, and where there is no avoiding both and where our actions can determine whether a greater or lesser evil obtains should we not plainly always opt for the lesser evil? And is it not obviously a greater evil that all those other innocent people should suffer and die than that the fat man should suffer and die? Blowing up the fat man is indeed monstrous. But letting him remain stuck while the whole group drowns is still more monstrous.

The consequentialist is on strong moral ground here and if his reflective moral convictions do not square with either certain unrehearsed or certain reflective particular moral convictions of human beings, so much the worse for such common-sense moral convictions. One could even usefully and relevantly adapt an argument of Donagan's here. Consequentialism of the kind I have been arguing for provides so persuasive 'a theoretical basis for common morality that when it contradicts some moral intuition, it is natural to suspect that intuition, not theory, is corrupt'.[16] Given the comprehensiveness, plausibility and overall rationality of consequentialism, it is not unreasonable to override even a deeply felt moral conviction if it does not square with such a theory, though, if it made nonsense or overrode the bulk of or even a great many of our considered moral convictions, that would be another matter indeed.

The case of the dispensable oldster, case 2, and the case of *der Übermensch* on a life raft, case 3, take a treatment similar to that of the fat man. In case 2 we surely violate the principle that the direct intention of the death of an innocent person is never justifiable. But where the old man himself is not willing to make the sacrifice which reflective morality requires and where the death of four other younger and very much needed people would result along with his own death, his being forced to go overboard seems to me to be a grim moral necessity. Yet it does violate a moral principle that certain Christian absolutists hold to be a principle which can never be overridden.

In actual practice, morally conscientious people would certainly hold on to the last possible moment and it is necessary in this endeavour to save everyone's life that they should take very considerable risks which might lead to the swamping

of the raft and the losing of everyone's life. That consequentialists argue that people must be prepared to take such
extreme risks, indicates that, while reasoning as consequentialists here in accordance with the principle of the lesser evil, they
have not abandoned the principle of respect for persons or
abandoned fairness or acceptance of universalizability. From
their moral point of view a desperate effort must be made to
save the man's life. And when and if it becomes undeniably
evident that all will perish if someone is not sacrificed, the old
man is not just selected out arbitrarily. There is a universalizable reason why he is selected rather than someone else and
there are humane reasons why it should be the sick old man
rather than a mother with five small children. Anti-conse-
quentialists often point to the inhumanity of people who will
sanction such killing of the innocent, but cannot the compli-
ment be returned by speaking of the even greater inhumanity
conjoined with evasiveness of those who will allow even more
death and far greater misery and excuse themselves on the
ground that they did not intend the death and misery but
merely forbore to prevent it? In this context such reasoning
and such forbearing to prevent seems to me to constitute a
moral evasion. I say it is evasive because rather than steeling
himself to do what is morally required here, though in normal
circumstances it would be a horrible and vile act, the anti-
consequentialist allows, when he has the power to prevent it,
a situation which is still many times worse.

In case 3, *der Übermensch* on a liferaft, we have a case where
I would argue that morally speaking it is essential that the
cancer-cure genius save himself even if that means he must
sacrifice the other innocent man. Note that he is not only
willing to kill an innocent man but that, from an Anscombean
point of view, he compounds the felony by being willing to
kill the innocent to save himself. However, this is a biased
characterization of the situation, for he is not willing to kill
the innocent just to save himself; he is willing to save himself

at the expense of another man because he has very good reason to believe that he and he alone in the forseeable future holds the key to a solution which will make death from cancer a thing of the past. Moreover, it is not that he denies human rights. He does not think that his life is intrinsically more valuable than the other man's life, but only that it is instrumentally more valuable. Everything else being equal, he has no more right to life than does the other man. But everything else is not equal. One man holds in his hands the key to saving thousands and perhaps millions of lives and untold dreadful suffering while the other does not. Since this is so, it is again a moral necessity rather than a moral monstrosity that this *Übermensch* kill the plain man, if they both cannot be saved and the plain man will not sacrifice himself. (*Übermenschen* of exactly that type in that type of situation must do the same thing.)

My consequentialist reasoning about cases 1, 2 and 3 is often resisted on the grounds that it starts a very dangerous precedent. People rationalize wildly and irrationally in their own favour in such situations. Moreover, it is rarely (if ever) the case that one actually gets a situation even approximating the situation of *der Übermensch* on the liferaft. There are very few such genuinely indispensable men, but most people under such duress will come up with ersatz reasons for affording themselves special treatment. And very frequently if people will put their wits to work or just endure, such admittedly monstrous actions, done to prevent still greater evils, will turn out to be unnecessary. Dudley and Stevens, who made a meal of their cabin boy when adrift at sea without food, were rescued not long after their revolting meal. The general moral principles surrounding bans on killing the innocent are so strong and play such a crucial role in the ever-floundering effort to humanize the savage mind—savage as a primitive and savage again as a contemporary in industrial society—that it is of the utmost social utility, it can be argued, that such bans against

killing the innocent not be called into question in any practical
manner by consequentialist reasoning.

However, in arguing in this way, my theistic and/or
deontological absolutist has now plainly shifted his ground and
he is himself arguing on consequentialist grounds that we must
treat certain non-consequentialist moral principles as absolute
(as principles which can never in fact, from a reasonable moral
point of view, be overridden, for it would be just too disastrous
to do so). But now he is on my home court and my reply is
that there is no good evidence at all that in the circumstances
I characterized in cases 1, 2 and 3 that overriding these
deontological principles would have this disastrous effect. I am
aware that they could set a bad precedent by being extended
to other doubtful cases. But my telling of little stories in some
detail and my contrasting of cases 1, 2 and 3, on the one hand,
with 4, 5, 6 and 7, on the other, was done in order to make
evident the type of situation, with its attendant rationale, in
which the overriding of those deontological principles can be
seen clearly to be justified and the type of situation in which
this does not obtain and why. My point was to specify the
situations in which we ought to override our common-sense
moral convictions about those matters as well as the situations
in which we are not so justified or at least it is not clear which
course of action is justified.[17]

If people are able to be sufficiently clear-headed about these
matters, they can see that there are relevant differences between
the two sorts of case. The cases involving rationalization are
quite different from 1, 2 and 3, but it was with these latter
situations where I was (and still am) defending a departure
from the dictates of common-sense morality. But I was also
carefully guarding against extending such moral radicalism, if
such it should be called, to other and more doubtful cases.
Unless solid empirical evidence can be given that such a moral
radicalism, if it were to gain a toehold in the community,
would overflow destructively and inhumanely into the other

doubtful and positively unjustifiable cases, nothing will undermine the correctness of my consequentialist defence of moral radicalism in the contexts in which I defended it.

I have tried here by commenting on my seven exemplary tales to establish that criticisms such as Anscombe's and Donagan's of consequentialism and thus indirectly of the normative ethic I argued for in Chapter Three were not well taken. Clear-headed and humane consequentialists will often stick to common-sense moral principles even, when viewed superficially, they appear to be unjustifiable on consequentialist grounds. However, viewed more circumspectly, it is plausible to maintain that they have a consequentialist rationale. (Cases 4, 5, 6 and 7 were of that type.) But there are other situations in which consequentialists should challenge common-sense moral responses and advocate what I call a form of moral radicalism. That is indeed difficult to do for our own very visceral responses are against it. I feel almost guilty and at least queasy in arguing as I do, as if I were advocating not only something which may indeed contain conceptual blunders (hardly something to feel guilty about) but also something which is morally monstrous or at least perverse. Yet surely the heart should work with the head. We know there are good psychological and moral reasons to have strong feelings about such common-sense moral principles because in the ordinary case they are surely principles to stand by.[18] But we feel equally strongly about unnecessary suffering and choosing the lesser evil. And our heads should tell us that what is morally appropriate in the ordinary case need not be so in the extraordinary case. My argument is that cases 1, 2 and 3 are just those extraordinary cases where we should become moral radicals. In both types of case our considered moral response in the face of the particular moral phenomena is, if it is a rational and humane response, a response which is compatible with and finds an architectonic rationale in my type of consequentialist normative ethic. That is, my moral theory accounts for such moral practices and no convincing grounds have been given for abandoning such a Humanism for theistic absolutism or some secular form of deontological absolutism.

V

The foregoing discussion makes it evident that under certain circumstances the concept of morality I have defended commits me to sanctioning and indeed even advocating violence toward certain innocent individuals. I abhor violence as much as any man and I doubly abhor the romanticizing of violence or, as was common in the nineteenth century, the romanticizing of war. It may indeed be true that violence under certain circumstances can be an effective cathartic. It may be for some a 'cleansing spirit' or, for some groups of downtrodden people, a way of attaining identity and cohesion. But when I argue that violence, including violence toward the innocent, may under certain circumstances be justified and indeed obligatory, it is not such considerations which prompt me, but the realization that in certain circumstances even greater and more extensive misery will result if violence, and indeed violence toward the innocent, is not accepted, albeit with a heaviness of heart.

To examine this radical claim of mine further and to make good my promissory note to discuss our realistic cases and to anticipate and void the criticism that what I call 'moral radicalism' is only plausible in desert island or quasi desert island situations, I shall discuss some realistic cases.

We spoke in the first section of this chapter of the deliberate bombing of civilian populations and of guerrilla warfare. As actual warfare goes, the deliberate bombings of civilian targets—the bombing of Dresden is a good example—are often senseless and wanton acts of terror in no way justifiable. But consider the bombing in the Second World War of a German residential area housing workers in a strategic munitions factory and keep in mind the need to bring the war to a quick and decisive end in order to halt the slaying and brutalizing of millions of people in concentration camps. The moral case for such bombing seems indeed to be a very strong one. Yet it is plainly (consider the children) violence directed in part against innocent people. To say we do not directly intend their death, if we are acting as moral agents, is indeed true. We want the bombs to kill or injure their parents so as to stop the operation of the munitions factory. (The munitions factory is underground so we cannot bomb it directly.) We do not—and cannot from a humane point of view—want the children to be injured or to die. We also know or have very good reason to believe that many children and other wholly innocent people will be killed and yet we deliberately engage in such an action. We are, direct intentions or second intentions or no, overriding the moral principle that one is never justified in killing the innocent. We do it by an appeal to the principle that suffering is evil and that where it cannot be avoided we should choose the lesser suffering. It is true that the innocent in no way deserve to suffer. We cannot rightly speak of their just suffering. In fact, their suffering is unjust. But while justice is a central moral consideration, it is not the only relevant moral consideration and sometimes the claims of justice, where acting on them would cause great misery, should be set aside. In such circumstances, the innocent must suffer undeservedly because, unless they do suffer, a far greater total suffering will ensue.

We should ask those absolutists who say that it is always wrong to inflict suffering on the innocent whether they would be willing to say that it would have been wrong (unjustified and unjustifiable) for the Allies to have followed out the request of the underground and have bombed Auschwitz. By so bombing it, innocent people (some people enslaved in the concentration camps) would have been killed and the bombers would have known or have had every good reason to believe that such people would be killed; but in killing some through the bombing of the grounds, some further thousands of innocent people could have been saved. If this were indeed so—as it seems evident—would it not indeed have been the humane and right thing to do? Or would it have been wrong to have assassinated Hitler—if this was the way one's opportunity came—by throwing a grenade into a crowd where innocent people (including children who were there with their parents) would have been killed as well? To assert that such acts are never morally justifiable, are categorically not to be done, is, I submit, to call in question the very humanity (assuming he clearly understood the implications of his position) of such a Christian and/or deontological absolutist. To be such a moral fanatic that one will insist on acting in accordance with such deontological principles, come what may, is to hold a morally monstrous view. It is the implications of such an absolutism which is monstrous and not, as it is too frequently alleged, the implications of a consequentialism which incorporates an independent principle of justice.

NOTES

[1] Donagan, Alan, 'Is There a Credible Form of Utilitarianism?' and McCloskey, H. J., 'A Non-Utilitarian Approach to Punishment' in Bayles, Michael D. (ed) (1968), *Contemporary Utilitarianism*, New York: Anchor Doubleday

[2] Anscombe, Elizabeth (1957), 'Modern Moral Philosophy', *Philosophy*, pp 16–17

[3] Ryan, Alan (1968), 'Review of Jan Narveson's *Morality and Utility*', *Philosophical Books*, vol. IX, no. 3, p 14

[4] In actual life we seldom have the certainty, hypothesized here, about what will happen. How could they be so certain that they would not be rescued or that the loss of one man would make such a difference about capsizing? A recognition of this strengthens the utilitarian case. See Sprigge, T. L. S., 'A Utilitarian Reply to Dr McCloskey' in Bayles, Michael D. (ed) (1968), *Contemporary Utilitarianism*, New York: Anchor Doubleday

[5] Foot, Phillipia (1967), 'The Problem of Abortion and the Doctrine of the Double Effect', *The Oxford Review* (Trinity), pp 5–15

[6] Later I shall show that there are desert island circumstances—that is, highly improbable situations—in which such serum-making might be a moral necessity. But also I shall show what little force desert island cases have in the articulation and defence of a normative ethical theory.

7 'Everyone' here is used distributively. That is to say, I am talking about the interests of each and every one. In that sense everyone's interests need to be considered.

8 Donagan, op. cit., p 189

9 T. L. S. Sprigge argues in such a manner. See Sprigge, op. cit.

10 Donagan, op. cit., p 194

11 There is considerable recent literature about whether it is possible to derive moral claims from non-moral claims. See Hudson, W. D. (ed) (1969), *The Is-ought Question*, London: Macmillan.

12 Anscombe, Elizabeth (1967), 'Who is Wronged?', *The Oxford Review* (Trinity), pp. 16–17

13 In a neglected but important essay, W. D. Falk has made us keenly aware of what reason can and cannot do about such moral surds. See his 'Moral Perplexity', *Ethics*, vol. 66, January 1956

14 Donagan, op. cit., pp 199–200

15 Again, I am not asserting that we would have enough fortitude to assent to it were the roles actually reversed. I am making a conceptual remark about what, as moral beings, we must try to do and not a psychological observation about what we can do.

16 Donagan, op. cit., p 198

17 I have spoken, conceding this to the Christian absolutist for the sake of the discussion, as if (1) it is fairly evident what our common-sense moral convictions are here and (2) that they are deontological principles taken to hold no matter what the consequences. But that either (1) or (2) is clearly so seems to me very much open to question.

18 I do not mean to suggest that I am giving a blanket defence of our common-sense morality. That is one of the last things I would want to do. Much of what we or any other tribe take to be common-sense morality is little better than a set of magical charms to deal with our social environment. But I was defending the importance of such cross-culturally ubiquitous moral principles as 'one ought not to harm the innocent' or 'promises ought to be kept'. However, against Christian absolutists of the type I have been discussing, I take them to be *prima facie* obligations. This means that they always hold *ceteris paribus*; but the *ceteris paribus* qualification implies that they can be overridden on occasion. On my account, appeal to consequences and considerations of justice and respect for persons determines on which occasions they may be overridden.